2/2
£4-50

CW01636606

HARNESS RACING
IN THE UK

HARNESS RACING IN THE UK

Stella Havard

Whittet Books

This book is dedicated to Santana Lad and Stoneriggs Herbie (and Gwyne Higgins!) for all the 'moments of pleasure'.

TITLE PAGE ILLUSTRATION *Horses lining up for the start of the intermediate race at Almeley.*

First published 1994
Text © 1994 by Stella Havard
Whittet Books Ltd, 18 Anley Road, London W14 0BY

All rights reserved

Design by Paul Saunders

The right of Stella Havard to be identified as the author of this work has been asserted in accordance with the Copyright, Designs and Patents Acts 1988

British Library Cataloguing in Publication Data
A catalogue record for this book is available from the British Library

ISBN 1 873580 12 6

Diagram on page 23 by Peter Davies
The author and publishers are grateful to the following for permission to reproduce photographs (those not acknowledged are the author's own) that appear on the pages as listed: Clem Dodd, 74, 75, 85, 87, 125, 127; Mike Gibbons, 10, 25, 27, 49, 53, 57; James Griffith Photography, 77; Iain C. McLaren, 41, 45, 69, 70, 79, 84, 97, 113, 123, 139; Photosport (Cymru), title page, 9, 13, 14, 17, 28, 31, 33, 42, 46, 50/51, 57, 58, 59, 60, 63, 66, 67, 72, 80, 82, 83, 93, 100, 103, 108, 110, 114, 115, 117, 130, 132, 135

Typeset by John Saunders
Printed and bound by Bath Press

Contents

Acknowledgments

My heartfelt appreciation to Gareth Bowen, Anne Brophy and Oz Bryan, without whom this book would never have got 'off and pacing'. And many more have cheerfully assisted in the production, to whom I am eternally grateful, notably: Ian Armstrong, Carole Auld, Russ Andrew, Eric Beard, Ralph Bailey, Jack Bousefield, Wayne Bird, George Coward, Nora Coles, Dick Clifford, Les Coward, Peter Davies, Clem Dodd, Ian, Maureen, George & William Drysdale, Jack Dowie, Carl Davies, Debbie Dyer, Brian Davies, Paul & Mandy Evans, Wendy Fairclough, Steve Flook, Mike Gibbons, James Griffith, Gwyne & Brenda Higgins, Paul Havard, Alan Haythornthwaite, Sophie Harrison, Joanna Howarth, Dennis Hardwick, John Hansford, Edward Hart, Chris & Muriel Jenkins, Derek & Phyllis James, Angela Jones, J.S. Jones, Raymond Jenkins, Bob Kennedy, Mike Lord, Geraint Lewis, Jenny Lechmere, Terry Laventure, Tom Menzies, Iain McLaren, Jackie McGuire, Gary Maw, Jim McInally, Robert Millichap, Richard Muddle, Helen Morton, Richard Owens, Ian Pimlott, Brendan Paterson, Conway Price, Roy Pugh, Megan Royle, Brian & Tracy Reynolds, Arthur & Evelyn Slack, Dot Smith, Mike Strickland, Heulwen Thomas, John & Elizabeth Towe, Harry Taylor, Pete Turner, Maynir Thomas, Gary Wakefield, Paul Williams, Mick Wilcox, Mick Yeomans and particularly to Annabel Whittet for the opportunity to highlight the sport which provides thousands of enthusiasts with so much pleasure. Many thanks!

1

Introduction to Harness Racing

The vast majority of people in the UK have little or no idea of what harness racing actually is. Strangely, though Britain is the recognized birthplace of the ancestors of the best harness racing stock in the world, the sport has received little public attention from within these shores. Yet in America, Australasia and Europe, the breeding and racing of 'trotters' and 'pacers' (the two types of horse used) is a major industry. Commonly referred to as 'trotting' in this country (despite the fact that most runners are laterally gaited 'pacers'), it is in fact a thrilling form of racing where horses maintain a non-galloping gait whilst driven by men or women poised on the seat of a lightweight cart called a 'sulky'. From April until October on the grass circuits, continuing until early January on the hard tracks, most races are run over the distance of a mile, with the object of breaking the two-minute barrier. (Golden Dale currently holds the British mile record with Alan Haythornthwaite at 1 minute, 59.4 seconds.) As a spectacle, it is enhanced by the fact that most of the circuits are only half a mile, so that the onlooker is never far from the melee of flying legs and wheels, and cannot possibly remain unmoved by the excitement of the action.

In 1992, the sport began to jog quietly out of the twilight. At last there was a chance of ditching the undeserved and outmoded image that racing with sulkies had somehow gained. Respectability was imminent! This was mainly due to the Jockey Club approaching the British Harness Racing Club, which is the governing body of the sport, with a view to affiliating the two hundred plus meetings that take place every year. Despite the members agreeing in principle, the deal on offer at that time was not attractive, and negotiations were put on a back burner, but the realization that the sport enjoyed so much and so quietly by so many was a saleable commodity caused a minor revolution. The television company, S4C, began to broadcast racing live from Tir Prince Raceway in North Wales; Lingfield Park racecourse in Sussex held meetings which attracted trotters from across the Channel and a new purpose-built floodlit track was opened at Dunstall Park, Wolverhampton racecourse, where harness racing would coexist with its Thoroughbred counterpart. At last the unsung heroes of the circuits began to receive their rightful recognition.

Many people labour under the misapprehension that harness racing is a new sport. In fact, it has been practised widely for well over a century, and there were pictures and reports of trotting meetings held in Alexandra Park in *The Graphic* in the 1870s. In America harness racing can be traced back over 3,000 years, though records only began to be kept in 1806.

In the past there have been hard tracks such as Prestatyn, Manchester, Chasewater and Kendal which have come and gone for various reasons (usually money) but currently there are five established circuits in the UK: Tir Prince Raceway in North Wales, Corbiewood Stadium in Scotland, Amman Valley Trotting Club in South Wales and York Raceway in England cater for the speedy professionals of the sport, and Dunstall Park, Wolverhampton, opened for business in 1994.

There are also thirty-odd grass circuits dotted all over Britain, though there is a high concentration of tracks in the Welsh Borders and in the north of England. Wreningham, in Norfolk, boasts a permanent grass track with a surface akin to a billiard table, and new clubs are now being formed to provide meetings in the southern counties.

The sport seems to breed characters, and, though some of them are disparaging about the upward direction that their sport is taking because they are happy to be heroes in their own backyards, most are keen that their expertise will at last reap a decent reward. 'We have to go forward,' commented Ammanford-based driver, Tony Richards. 'Times change. The Morris 8 was the car to have in 1937, but it would have a job to keep up nowadays!'

Perhaps because of the harness, the sport sometimes looks and sounds rather complicated, but, once conversant with the basics, it is actually very straightforward. I hope the following explanations will unravel some of the mystery.

Trotting is a diagonal gait where the left fore and right hind legs move forward in unison, followed by the right fore and left hind. Though trotting is the only gait permitted by harness racing authorities in other European countries, **pacing** is the dominant gait in the UK, as it is in America and Australasia.

Pacing is a natural gait for some breeds of horse (and giraffes) and is

Who could remain unmoved by the action? Gary Bond and Flyn, 67-year- old Tony Hammonds and Little Erster at Walton.

where front and back legs on the same side move forward simultaneously; it is approximately three seconds a mile faster than 'square' trotting.

Most harness racehorses in Britain are **Standardbreds**. This breed can be traced back to English Thoroughbred bloodlines, and therefore, like the Thoroughbred, is descended from the Byerly Turk, the Godolphin Arab and the Darley Arabian. Because of the emphasis on speed, and because American Standardbreds are some of the fastest, there is currently a very strong American influence on the British breeding of the Standardbred. The name was adopted for the breed in 1879 when it was considered by the American Trotting Register that it was a fair 'standard' for horses to be able to trot or pace the mile in 2 minutes, 30 seconds.

Though some horses pace completely naturally (which is referred to as 'free-legged' pacing), in races they mostly wear light loops made of plastic or leather around their legs with straps that connect the legs on the same side, which help them find their best length of stride. These aids are called '**hopples**' (or 'hobbles') and are suspended over the horse's withers, back and rump by '**hangers**'. Even if a horse paces naturally, it

The start car follows the runners and the official starter also acts as a steward.

is unlikely that he would consistently do so at racing speed without the hopples to encourage him to maintain his gait. The horse is unaware that he is able to pace faster than he can gallop (as Standardbreds generally can) and, until he is educated to the fact, he is likely to canter just like any other horse when asked to speed up without the hopples. '**Hitting**' the hopples helps to instil the habit to pace rather than '**break**'. Trotters, of course, do not require hopples (unless as some obscure remedy for gait problems in other countries), but driving a trotter is a real art since keeping them balanced is crucial to prevent them 'breaking'. This is a term used when a horse deviates from its proper pacing or trotting gait, generally by galloping. Because the rhythm is interrupted, this actually slows the horse down fairly abruptly, so that it could be a danger to the horses behind. Thus a 'breaker' must be pulled to the outside until it is 'back on its legs', but if it breaks consistently, or is in a break crossing the line, it will be disqualified from the race.

Most races in the UK are commenced with a '**start car**'. This is a motor vehicle with metal 'wings' on the back that guide the horses who are drawn 1–5 off the gate (the five positions directly behind the gate). The official starter usually stands on the back of the vehicle to give his instructions, and the 'under starter's orders' signal is usually conveyed by a flashing green light or a white flag. If he is unhappy about the positioning or rhythm of the horses, the starter refuses to release them and a false start is called.

The runners gather in their correctly handicapped positions some way before the starting post, and the gate gains speed so that they are dispatched at about 30 m.p.h. at which point the gate usually leaves the track. A horse is currently handicapped ten yards for each victory to a maximum of eighty yards, and a driver is expected to correctly judge his own 'mark', i.e. the distance he is supposed to be behind the gate. The 'gate' horses have no handicap deficit, currently termed Class 000. A common practice to aid the 'back' drivers, i.e. those off the furthest handicap marks, used to be a trail rope calibrated with coloured flags, but luckily this is mainly discontinued as occasionally the horses drawn on position one, next to the rails, were unsettled by the noise or sight of the rope on the inside.

Getting away from the start is always a highly critical point in the race for horses and drivers, as jockeying for position to take the first bend is often crucial to the result. Being held on the outside, which is making a horse race so much further, is called '**getting parked**', but, though this is undesirable, it is perhaps infinitely better than the opposite of being '**in the box**' where a horse is trapped on the inside with others all around it and has no room to make a run. Obviously, driver tactics are crucial in a race! Though harness racing can often seem to the spectator like something out of *Ben Hur*, there are very strict rules regarding clearance and safety, and accidents are unlikely. Naturally, due to the speed, when one does happen, it appears very dramatic, but it is a pleasing fact that serious injury to either horse or driver is rare indeed. And another fact is that those who become involved with the sport on any level become thoroughly hooked and remain addicted for life – ask any participant!

2

Buying the Basics

Once hooked on the spectacle of the equine athletes with brightly-silked drivers poised on fragile sulkies, the average equestrian usually becomes seized with the urge to sample the excitement personally. This even happens to people largely unconnected to horses. Respected trainer and breeder, Ian Drysdale, visited Corbiewood Stadium purely out of curiosity twenty-odd years ago with no knowledge at all of what to expect, and was inspired immediately to purchase a yearling, and 'picked it up as he went along'. Ralph Bailey, one of the leading owners in Wales and the West, spotted a poster advertising a fixture and also went along just to see what on earth harness racing actually was. He, too, was moved to become involved but had no experience beyond his daughters' gymkhana ponies. He eventually discovered that there were public trainers who produced harness racehorses for a living, and was put in touch with one, Steve Flook, in Herefordshire. Taking advice, Ralph purchased Cover Note and two years later took the Leading Owner award in the region. These are only a couple of examples of the effect the sport can have on the unwary!

One of the main attractions of harness racing is that it is a 'hands on' activity. Age has little relevance to prowess as a driver and, provided the fifteenth birthday has been attained, there is little impediment. At the other end of the scale, there are several 'veterans' on the circuits regularly proving that age and cunning more than compensate for youth and strength as they drive good winners. In fact when Stan Harrison drives his game and consistent stallion, Cool Teddy, their combined ages are not a million miles away from the century! Other drivers well over the age of consent who are no strangers to the winners' enclosure are celebrated Welshman, Bill Edwards, Bristol-based farrier, Mike Strickland, Herefordshire dairy-farmer, Gwyne Higgins, Scottish publican, Alex McDonald and the permanently youthful-

Neither sex nor age a bar to drivers! Sally Teeboon (Greenfold Kerrie) leads 66-year-old Stan Harrison (Cool Teddy) at Upton.

looking Johnny Blissett, among others. Nor is there any disadvantage to the female gender in the sport, though there are fewer lady drivers than men. Evelyn Slack, who is the currently the senior lady driver, won the 1993 National Pacing Derby with Stoneriggs Merc and has the distinction of being a grandmother. Her daughter, Diane Sayer, is also a force to be reckoned with on the sulky seat, as are Helen Morton, Alex Lees, Sian Gresley-Jones, Clare and Diane Bousefield, Sally Teeboon, Megan and Joanne Taff, Nicky Cabb, Debbie Birbeck, Andrea Young and Pam Haythornthwaite, to name but a few of the ladies who race on UK circuits.

Once smitten with the sport, how does one go about actually purchasing a Standardbred with a view to having some fun on the way to the winners' circle? Harness racing can seem a closed shop to the uninitiated. It isn't possible to open the pages of a local newspaper and scan the prospective purchases in the columns there as one could for every other equestrian discipline. (Though John Mac was lucky enough to buy the prolific winner, Jimmy's Decision, from an advert in the *Farmers Guardian*). And there is only one official sale a year, staged at Builth Wells in October by Russell, Baldwin & Bright Markets, though there may be a couple of youngstock reduction sales at the bigger studs. So for the true newcomer, it can all seem slightly

One of the leading drivers at Tir Prince Raceway, Johnny Blissett, who has been gracing the circuits for many years, driving Sly Lyss.

daunting. But the horses are there to be bought, mostly privately from studs or trainers, it's just a case of asking around. And one thing is certain, the sport is bristling with people only too willing to give the benefit of their advice; mainly because this involves one of their greatest vices – talking! Usually at great length.

The *Harness Racing Calendar*, the official publication of the BHRC (British Harness Racing Club), which is sent to all licence holders and is available on subscription from the headquarters at Dyserth at £10 per annum, often contains advertisements of horses and equipment for sale. The various other associations mostly produce their own newsletters which will also contain horses, etc., on offer in the locality.

In comparison to Thoroughbred bloodstock, harness racehorses are not expensive, though of course the good ones are not bought for peanuts. Much will depend on what you want to achieve. But a horse that will provide a lot of fun without breaking track records will cost from £900–£2,000. In comparison, for the equivalent schoolmaster/fun horse on the National Hunt scene, even in the current depressed trade due to the recession, one would have to pay out anything from 4,000–15,000 guineas.

Breeding, of course, is the key to speed in any form of racing. As founder of the legendary Saunders Stud, J. S. Jones so wisely observed, 'You can't *put* speed into 'em.' So if you're going to have a horse professionally trained to win decent races, a good-sized (but not overgrown), well bred yearling without any faults of conformation is the usual bet. The trainer you have selected (probably from watching his charges perform on the track) will usually do this business for you, break the animal during the winter, then produce it to race as a two-year-old. How much it does at this age varies according to the horse, trainer and owner, but it is not recommended to over-race a two-year-old. If you want more runs, go for an older horse. This also applies if you intend to train and drive yourself. Old-stager, Gwyne Higgins, wisely advises newcomers, 'You want one that knows his job, a youngster wouldn't be a pleasure to you.' And indeed, there are plenty of experienced horses who have perhaps found their handicap levels who would be ideal schoolmasters. No matter how well versed in other facets of the equestrian world, a new driver piloting a 'green' horse would be too much the blind leading the blind. Square trotters are becoming more popular as their chances to race increase and there are usually some for sale through the executives of the major raceways, but a trotter is not recommended as a novice drive. The following advice is mainly geared towards pacers, purely because they form the majority of runners in the UK.

The studs and breeders often have fields full of youngsters for sale. The Drysdale family, who currently stand the two top class stallions, Fleet Decision and Armbro Mystic, at Forest Mill in Scotland, happily show any interested parties the stock which roams their hundreds of well farmed acres and will give straightforward, unbiased advice. The bunches of foals, yearlings and older horses gallop eagerly to greet their visitors, who are spoiled for choice and leave with their heads spinning from recited pedigrees and performances. These horses are all bred to win, but, as Ian wryly remarks, a youngster with a brilliant future looks no different from a mediocre one at this stage. Seeing them in a bunch is always a help, because you can see whether the horse is confident, having learned to hold its own among the group, which will mean that on the track it will be unaffected by the scrimmage around it. Also, it is easier to watch a youngster move in these natural surroundings, and its attitude will give an indication of its temperament. Most trainers will agree that those with the most spirit, who are sometimes difficult to educate, generally make the best racehorses, because they never give in under pressure. But, of course, horses make fools of us all, and there are exceptions where a laid back animal will not waste any precious energy until the chips are down, and then gives his all and beats the spirited ones.

Whatever the age of the Standardbred to be purchased, it is vital that the conformation is basically correct, particularly the limbs. Any fault or weakness that may cause the legs to deviate in any way is sure eventually to result in '**interference**' (where a horse strikes himself with his own feet, knee-knocking, cross-firing, etc.). Though these problems can often be remedied by careful shoeing, remember, you can get enough trouble without buying it to start with. Though Standardbreds suffer relatively little leg trouble compared with their Thoroughbred counterparts, their problems are usually of a different nature. Joints and pedal-bones suffer most on the hard tracks, and it is not recommended for pasterns to be too upright or they will not be efficient 'shock absorbers', nor for shoulders to be too 'slabby' and straight. And the old adage, 'No foot, no horse' is truer than ever for an animal which will be striking miles of track with power and speed in his racing career. As with the purchasing of any horse, most of it is down to sound commonsense, and if in doubt get advice from a vet (but make sure it is one fully conversant with pacers, as those unfamiliar with the rolling, lateral action often imagine lameness where there is none). Obviously, for the novice driver, temperament is of prime concern, though most Standardbreds are pretty straightforward in this respect. If possible, try to watch the horse taking part in a race (you will just have to bite the bullet and pay more for him if he wins!), particularly if you intend to pilot him yourself. Pay special attention to how he behaves in the preliminaries and behind the start car, which is where those who do not handle the excitement 'boil over'. If you can't attend a race day, watch him being harnessed up and worked out at home, and 'get behind him' yourself. All tracks except Musselburgh are on the left rein (anti-clockwise), so make sure you try him this way round at a reasonable rate of knots to ensure he does not 'hang' (lean to one side or the other) on the bends. Take special note of how he leaves the yard to go to the training ground; if he is slightly out of love with the job, you may well be able to sweeten him up with a change of routine and surroundings, but if he is really nappy and reluctant, he will be more trouble than he is worth, and no fun will be had by anybody. The very worst nappers '**deck**' themselves (throw themselves on the ground) in protest, though any horse that develops this habit usually becomes notorious on the scene and you will probably have been warned by at least fifteen different advisers not to touch it with a barge pole. But keep your eye open for scrapes and grazes on the animal, and for any broken carts and shafts that happen to be in the yard.

Once their speed is no longer competitive on a hard track, horses are sometimes changed to grass, when they can go on to a great age if well looked after. Many people have the – erroneous – idea that harness racehorses are incapable of performing in any other equestrian sphere once they have retired from the track. This prejudice seemingly stems from the notion that a

Seasoned campaigner, Gwyne Higgins, with Stoneriggs Herbie at Walton.

pacer cannot trot or canter, which of course is complete nonsense. Turn one out in the field and he will cavort and gallop just like any other. There will of course be times when a seasoned horse will pace through choice, but with normal flat work, he will generally lose it as his dominant gait. Standardbreds are wonderfully agile and athletic, and have tremendous scope when jumping. Former world show-jumping champion, Jappeloup, a little French horse, was in fact trotting-bred, and Mark Todd's Olympic show-jumping ride, Double Take, is also by a 'trotter'. In New Zealand, harness-racing stock is often coupled with the Thoroughbred to produce a performance horse, as in many European countries. But the British have been slow to utilize the advantages of the Standardbred, though the breed is beginning to make a real impression in the sport of endurance riding, where their stamina, speed and outstanding toughness making them ideal for the demands required.

The even temperament of the Standardbred horse makes him eminently suitable as a 'rider', though a pacer should not be encouraged to learn to jump during his racing days lest he start leaping shadows, etc., on the circuit; many pacers have later found an enjoyable alternative career under saddle. Gwyne Higgins sold the roan pacer, Trixie Direct, as a 'rider', and, renamed the Hooded Crow, he went from complete novice to Grade 'A' in minimum time, and exchanged hands for an astronomical sum. Sir Edward unfortunately lost interest in racing, but his owner, Charles Sanders switched him to the saddle, and he now happily hunts and has even competed in the fearsome sport of team chasing. Santana Lad, who had been originally purchased as a 'schoolmaster' for the circuits, introduced three new drivers to the exhilaration of the winners' enclosure before making a name for himself and Paul Havard across country and in show-jumping speed classes. So don't worry about your Standardbred being relegated to the 'scrap heap', when his racing days are over, he will have plenty of options.

Successful pacer, Santana Lad, demonstrates with Paul Havard that Standardbreds can also win in other equestrian spheres. Pacers usually have great scope.

Once the deal has been done (and, like most horse people, harness racing folk adore haggling) with a horse that has been broken, there is a lot of information you need from the trainer: what length of hopple does it races in (measured from tip of front hopple loop to end of back hopple loop)? how many holes are they usually let out for daily jogging? is it shod in any particular way (there are a legions of possibilities here)? do the feet need any special attention? does it run best in blinkers, an open bridle or Kant-See-Baks (which are 'shades' that just prevent the horse from looking back at his driver)? is there any specific bit, overcheck or gadget (such as a head-pole) that is needed to produce optimum performance? Obviously, different trainers use different methods, but if you're feeling your way to start with, it is best not to start by changing things until you know a bit more about the horse and the job he must do! In America, each horse has a record card on which all these details are tabled, which is always passed on with it, and it would certainly be a boon if the system could be developed in the UK.

Apart from the obvious basic equipment that any horse would need, your newly purchased racehorse will require a set of harness and hopples. Every horse that goes into training takes its own set with it, which is a bit of a shock if you don't happen to be acquainted with the fact. Most people use plastic harness nowadays, and it can be bought through the aforementioned adverts, or from the suppliers who are invariably selling it at meetings. A complete set of new harness may cost around the £200 mark, though that is generally without bits, blinkers or reins, or the complete hopples, which are anything from £45–£60 a set. Many dealers may have the odd second-hand set, and most trainers may be able to help; 'doing a deal' is almost a compulsion with many of them.

The light racing sulky (usually referred to as a 'cart' or 'bike') can be obtained from the same sources, but with drivers often bringing over the more up-to-date models from America, it is frequently possible to pick them up second-hand. Brand new, the best makes of cart will cost in excess of a thousand pounds, but before you reach for the smelling salts, a perfectly serviceable second-hand one will be anything from £60–£400, depending on how skilled you are at bargaining. Again, asking around is surprisingly productive. Generally, horses are exercised in a heavier jogging cart, which is more durable than the racing one. The jogging cart is usually made of metal rather than wood, and is much cheaper.

Racing wheels are fairly expensive and can cost up to £120. These would not last long bumping around a field at home, and motorbike wheels from the local scrap yard are an adequate substitute for exercising. But the smart racing ones must have the compulsory safety discs in the centres. The wheels must be correctly aligned so that they track freely and balance with the driver's weight, causing no upward or downward pressure on the pad. Wider tyres are sometimes used on the grass tracks, usually with slightly less air. The harder surfaces of the raceways need a greater inflation, and a foot pump is a vital piece of equipment, not to mention a puncture repair kit! The correct-sized spanners for changing wheels and moving seats should also be nestled amongst the kit.

There is always much discussion about whether the weight of a driver makes a great deal of difference to a horse's performance. A heavy man (or woman) does not detract from the speed of a harness racehorse as much as a heavy jockey does to a Thoroughbred since, once the cart is moving, it is balanced and merely overcoming friction. Gloucestershire farrier and Class 'A' driver, Gary Wakefield, explains his theory by using the example of a loaded wheelbarrow, which, he claims, is easier to push than an empty one. But others contend that the only people who maintain that weight makes little difference are the overweight drivers. Certainly a good driver who is on the heavier side is better on the sulky seat than a lighter, less talented one. The strike rate of seasoned campaigner, Dave Taff, who has the physique of a front-row rugby player, but the hands of an angel and the brain of Pat Eddery, more than proves this. But in heavy conditions, there is no doubt at all that weight is a disadvantage, and it cannot be mere coincidence that the drivers at the top of the National Championship table are all on the sylph-like side.

If you are intending to drive your own horse, you will need an approved skull cap or headgear, and a set of racing colours made up, and you must register them with BHRC when paying your dues to become an owner and permit trainer. Horses now have to be registered to race yearly at Weatherbys Harness Racing Department, though the thirty pounds fee has to be made payable to the BHRC.

Once you have gained driving experience and become confident at handling horse and sulky, you must prove to the stewards that you are capable of doing the same at racing speed in public. The driving test used to be taken in a mock race, but the requirements are currently under review, and most test drivers now have to perform in a certain number of qualifying races. A 'qualifier' is a non-betting race usually staged prior to racing as an introduction for young and inexperienced horses. Before they are allowed into the racing system, where they usually begin in a maiden race, they must be capable of recording a certain time over the mile. This varies according to the track, but mostly on grass tracks it is in the region of two minutes, twenty-four seconds. If seasoned horses are running in a qualifier for a test, or to requalify after injury, they must 'trail' (or start) twenty yards behind the genuine 'babies'. A good knowledge of the rules and regulations of the sport (available from BHRC) is also vital for the learning driver, and, once the stewards are happy that you are safe to be let loose on the circuits, a driver 'C' licence may be applied for. All licences are issued with a registration number. Should you really get the bug and eventually wish to be upgraded, a class 'B' licence will be granted after two seasons of holding the 'C ' category, provided you have had at least 25 drives without incurring penalties for any major infringement, and have driven 5 winners, of which at least one must have been on a hard track. A class 'A' licence is the advanced/international category, and is the one required to drive in Classic races. Obviously, to be upgraded to 'A', the applicant needs to be very experienced, having driven a minimum of 16 wins from at least 25 outings on a hard track, and had at least 24 winning drives. The stewards, of whom at least three must support the upgrading, also have to examine the applicant's driving record and consider penalties incurred and the times achieved with a variety of horses.

Not counting the registration of your horse, which if you have been smart enough to buy at the right time will already have been paid for the year, becoming an owner/permit trainer/'C' driver will cost just over £57 for the various licences with BHRC.

As well as the harness, sulky, and the various boots and aids that your particular horse may require, one of the most vital pieces of equipment to a harness-racing enthusiast is a stopwatch. Study the species carefully, and you will note that all serious trainers, drivers and spectators seem to have one welded permanently into the palm of one hand. Thus they know exactly what speed over what distance a horse is capable of. Apart from being an essential piece of training equipment, the stopwatch forms the basis of most of the jargon in the harness racing world. Thus the description of a horse as, 'He's done two eights but I reckon he's got a two-four in 'im,' can be roughly translated into, 'Having already recorded a mile time of two minutes, eight seconds, I think he could do a time of two minutes, four seconds.' (Quite fast enough to frighten the living daylights out of the true novice driver!)

Once you've invested in a stopwatch, you have to face the fact that you are hooked on harness racing. But before you start trying to remember to press buttons as you fly past the starting post, it is wise to recall that the most important clock to a driver in the race is the one in his (or her) head.

3

Where on Earth do all These Straps Go . . . ?

Even someone reasonably well acquainted with things equestrian could be forgiven for feeling as if they have landed on another planet when handed a bundle of harness and hopples with which to dress a horse for the first time. Even the names are alien, but it's a comfort to find that many are merely familiar items masquerading under a different label; for example 'bell' boots are nothing more alarming than rubber overreach boots (worn on the front feet to protect the bulbs of the heels) and 'shin boots' are those usually called 'brushing boots' which protect the front tendons, though confusingly, the same boots on the hind legs (usually worn by square trotters) are known as 'scalping boots'. A rose by any other name . . .

Another thing that can throw the uninitiated is the habit of harness-makers to expect appropriate buckles to be used to accommodate more than one strap. Thus, when the unwary are wondering what on earth the strap that suspends the back hopple-hangers (or carriers) attaches to, the answer is the crupper-buckle. The same goes for those pondering where to fix the strap that suspends the shadow-roll (sheepskin noseband) on the bridle. It merely slides through the top buckle which holds the blinkers in place, on top of the strap already there. On reflection, it makes perfect sense, but can bewilder the straightforward recruits who expect one buckle per strap. Another natty little idea, usually found on the hopple-hangers or the overcheck, is the 'free' buckle. This is not sewn to anything to make altering lengths easier, and the same strap passes through it twice. These things may sound a little complicated on paper, but are perfectly comprehensible 'in the flesh'. Fore-warned is fore-armed!

Possibly because most people are accustomed to harnessing up with the horse tied to a lorry at the races, older horses are usually tacked up outside their stables. But even if dressing a horse inside his box, it is not

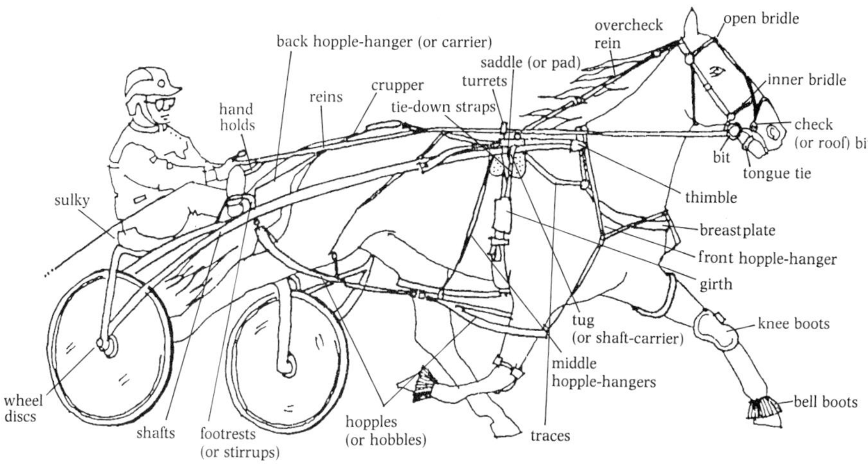

Basic harness used on a Standard bred pacer (tongue tie and boots optional).

recommended to put a 'blind' bridle (with blinkers) on until he has negotiated the doorway, as the restricted vision could impair his judgement and perhaps cause him to bang his hips as he walks through the narrow space. This presents no great problem since the bridle is generally the last piece of equipment to be put on before the cart is hitched. But trainer, Dennis Hardwick, advises that care should always be taken when leading an unknown horse through a doorway. Some mishap in the past can often cause him to rush wildly through, causing the handler to be either knocked over and/or trampled on.

As with all areas of equestrianism, there is more than one way of doing things, and everyone is of the opinion that their way is the *right* way. But there are some very definite rules that every serious trainer adheres to. Every horse should have his own set of harness and hopples that are adjusted correctly, and should not be altered to suit other horses. It sometimes takes months to get a horse going just right, and to forget to move buckles because tack has been used on something else is risking the undoing of a lot of time, sweat and patience. Aberystwyth trainer, Peter Davies, is a stout believer in his horses jogging in the same tack that they wear at the races so that the handler can gauge if anything needs changing, rather than them wearing unfamiliar kit to race. There is a lot to support this theory, though older horses usually have their hopples lengthened a couple of holes for slower work. And though there is a wagonload of gadgets available, these are best treated as a last resort. Everything that the horse wears should be comfortable. The driver wouldn't dream of going out for a race wearing a vest two sizes too small, and can hardly expect his charge to break the two-minute-mile barrier if he feels similarly uncomfortable. Plastic harness, which is so much easier to clean, now adorns most British tack rooms, but is apt to crack at the buckles in time and needs regular checking. It also stretches with use, so an eye should be kept on straps, and holes altered accordingly.

Practice makes perfect in all things, particularly harnessing up. The best advice for learning the art is to watch it being performed as much as possible. Most people put on the saddle (or pad) to begin the process, but one veteran driver was so superstitious that he would refuse to go out on the circuit behind any horse that was not dressed with the breastplate (or breast collar) as the first item. No doubt he was the kind of man who always pulled on his right sock before his left one every morning in the hope that this placated the gremlins of destiny! Whatever your routine, always remember to be deft and quiet, no horse will appreciate having his teeth banged by the bit, or his skin pinched by the girth, or the saddle (or pad) banged crudely onto his back.

The saddle and padding should 'sit' just behind the withers, and a firmly adjusted (but not overtight) crupper will prevent it from being pulled forward by the overcheck, the strap that keeps a horse's head up so that he is balanced in his stride. Harness horses are no different to any others and blow out when the girth is tightened, and it will need to be pulled up after a few minutes.

The breastplate should be positioned just under the lower end of the throat, since it must not restrict the windpipe in any way. It must also allow free movement of the shoulders, and once the traces have been wrapped around or passed through loops on the sulky shafts before being attached to lugs, it is not a bad idea to give an experimental pull on the breastplate just to check that the poor animal is not going to be half strangled. The front hopple-hanger (or carrier), which fits over the neck just in front of the withers and buckles at the breast, is worn on *top* of the breastplate.

The back hangers are clipped onto the crupper, while the two 'middle' ones are attached to the bottom strap which connects the crupper to the saddle. The 'self-righting' type of hopple hanger merely runs freely between these top and bottom straps. These are a bit of a nuisance during the tacking up and untacking processes as they pull through until the hopples on both sides are fastened onto them. Most people lift the front leg into the hopple

For the busy trainer and driver, a good back-up team is essential.

loop first, fastening the front strap whilst keeping the rear loop and connector tucked between their knees to keep the hands free. The point of the buckle tongue on the connector should always face forward. When the front loop is correctly fastened, the process should be repeated for the hind leg. The hopples themselves are a critical part of the gear. Their height and length are absolutely vital for a horse to produce his optimum performance, and it takes a very well gaited horse to pace consistently at racing speed without them. They should be adjusted to fit into the 'hollow' of the hind leg, running slightly downwards to just above the 'knot' on the foreleg. The correct length can be roughly estimated by measuring a hand's breadth between the front loop and the fore limb when the hopple is pulled snug against the hind leg. But make sure the horse is standing square, and not with his legs all over the place, to adjudge this. Most trainers smear a lubricant such as baby oil or talcum powder inside the hopples and the legs where the horse 'hits' them to minimize friction. Youngsters are often treated with surgical spirit in this region so that they resist chafing, but, like people, some have more sensitive skin than others. The hopples, like any boots that the horse wears, should be rinsed and wiped clean after every outing, especially on a hard track, lest small pieces of grit or dirt should damage the skin when they are next worn.

The bridle is usually put on just before the cart is hitched up. It is vital that the horse is comfortable around the head, and that the throatlash is not overtightened, or it will obstruct the windpipe when the horse most needs his breath at the business end of a race. A horse that doesn't concentrate on his job, or gawks about 'spooking', should wear blinkers. These should be linked by a nose-strap to prevent them being pulled away from the eyes by the action of the reins in the hurly-burly of a race. How much a horse needs to be 'closed down' (have his field of vision restricted) depends on his own behaviour on the track. But the novice driver should bear in mind that blinkers obscure the side vision; if ever you are in trouble, and it looks as if your horse is going to hit a rail or fence, your first instinct would be to pull him away and off the hazard, but in fact, if his head is turned towards it, he will see it and avoid it. But it is extremely rare for such a situation to occur, and usually only does so with very young, green animals.

Lazy horses are often sharpened up by blinkers, just as their Thoroughbred counterparts are, but, for some, 'Kant-See-Baks' are enough to keep their minds on the task in hand, just so they are not watching the driver instead of looking forward. The overcheck is a strap, attached either to a roof bit or to a chin-strap, which runs up the middle of the horse's face, through the browband and crownpiece, and is attached to the pad to keep the horse from lowering his head unduly during a race. It is mostly clipped up at the last minute when the horse is about to go out on the track, or out to jog. When the 'check' is not clipped up, it should never be allowed to swing free, but should be snapped onto the bit ring to prevent the metal clasp causing injury if the horse should throw his head up. Another thing that usually happens when the 'check' is unclipped is that the roof or check bit slackens in the horse's mouth and bangs against his teeth or gets spat out. Seasoned campaigner, Harry Perkins, remedies this problem by drilling extra holes in a pair of rubber bit-ring guards, so that both bits are passed through the rubber discs, which maintain the position of the roof bit even when the overcheck is loosened.

Generally, a horse is more likely to gallop with his head down, and most horses balance against the overcheck to find their stride and rhythm. With a young horse, it will be adjusted often until the ideal length is found. As in all facets of equestrianism, there are a multitude of different bits on offer, and the same old adage, 'Out of ten bits invented, there are nine for a man's head and one for a horse's mouth,' still applies. Again, try to keep things simple with the half-cheeked driving snaffle, but a rubber version suits a lot of horses, especially if they pull hard. (Legendary driver, Clem Dodd, advises that you should try not to fight a horse in a race, the more you pull, the

Plenty of length of rein is needed for walking behind the cart.

more he will.) Before changing bits or resorting to gadgets to help straighten a horse, get his teeth checked. The 'tooth doctor' can eliminate many basic problems such as sharp edges and wolf teeth, and should be summoned immediately if steering difficulties are encountered.

When actually 'putting the horse in the cart', the shafts are passed through the tugs, with the cups or thimbles fitted over the ends immediately to prevent them from sliding too far forward and digging into the horse's neck and frightening him. The tie-down straps from the girth are wrapped around the shafts, usually on both sides of the tugs to maintain their position. Again, there is always more than one way to skin a cat, and everyone seems to have their pet routine for this, so look, learn and decide for yourself. But most of them agree that it is dangerous to tie in the traces with the tie-downs; traces are usually attached to the shafts before tying down (though they usually pass through the loop), as releasing them would become more difficult in the event of an accident.

Because there are quite enough straps to be juggling with when hitching the cart, the reins are not usually attached until last. They are generally pulled through the turrets before being buckled onto the bit, and, when the horse is not being driven, they are normally looped around or through the nearside turret. The reins are a matter of personal taste. Some have webbing or rubber grips on them, and some pairs have 'ladders' where you can choose the best place to hold them without pre-setting the loop or grip. Most have plenty of length, which is needed when walking behind the cart, but it is an offence on the track to let them drag or dangle dangerously, and the best plan is to pass the ends over the sulky seat underneath the driver's rump.

Many horses, especially when fit, are on the tetchy side when being harnessed, almost as if they have to psyche themselves up. Thus they fasten their teeth on doors, wooden struts, etc., and often bite alarming chunks out of the same. (A wooden box on a lorry is a non-starter if you don't want it to look as though it has been attacked by rampant beavers by the end of the season!) Even the most gentlemanly individual is not above taking the odd

A new owner's dream: Cover Note, owned by Ralph Bailey, winner of 22 races to date.

pot as his hind feet are being lifted into the hopples, so be warned!

The racing sulky obviously has to suit both the horse and driver. The cart will be balanced best if it is close to the horse. However, big, long-striding horses will need longer shafts, as they sometimes catch the stirrups or even the wheel with their hind feet when fully extended on a bend. As designs of 'bike' improve on the American market, the top drivers tend to trade their carts in fairly regularly in the hope of finding extra seconds on the track. Many custom-build their own models to suit their own tastes. Mike Lord, who topped the UK drivers championship table in 1992 and 1993, has been contesting the circuits for twenty-five years. When he began his career at fifteen years of age, his legs were much too short to reach the stirrups (footrests) even when both they and the seat had been shortened as much as possible – his cart had to be modified considerably. Not that this detracted from his performance in any way, since his track debut resulted in his first win. His legs have certainly become a little longer since then.

But before blueing the housekeeping on a cart which appears to be a very good deal, check with BHRC that it is a make that has not been banned, even if it is a high-class American model. Also, ensure that there is a rear cross-piece joining the bars to which the seat is bolted, since this is a new requirement to enhance safety on the circuits.

A few of the top trainers have invested in 'slick-hitch' carts, where the shafts clip into a special harness designed for this type of cart. Top professional driver and trainer Jim McInally has several carts of this design and reports that they are well worth the outlay for the time, tension and bad temper that they save behind the scenes when he has a runner in each race. For a busy trainer and driver, a good back-up team is absolutely essential.

But whatever 'bike' you choose, don't put the cart before the horse. He is the most important item in the scheme of things, and the lightest, most expensive 'bike' in the world is useless if he does not perform happily in it. On race days, the different sets of harness, boots, etc., for each individual horse are usually transported in large bags. These may be anything from the super-smart leather or plastic variety with the trainer's logo on the outside to the large linen bags used by laundries. But the general idea is to keep all the equipment required for each horse together and easily transportable.

It is also a sound idea to protect the precious shafts on your cart during transportation, particularly if it is to be hung on the back of a lorry or trailer. Most people employ tubes of foam rubber, but even wrapping old travelling bandages around them is better than nothing.

Once you are familiar with everything, including your horse and his habits, the harnessing routine will become second nature. Until then, stay cool, take your time and don't get your traces in a twist!

4

Fit, not Fat!

Getting a horse fit for any activity requires good feeding coupled with adequate exercise. 'Stress without strain,' should be the guideline, and the acquired muscle should be based on a decent foundation of slow work over a period of time. Those who ride their harness horses tend to give them six to eight weeks of routine roadwork as a basis, but those who solely use a track jog endless slow miles to build up muscle fitness, progressing to shorter spells of fast work to prepare the wind for the demands of racing.

Young horses unaccustomed to the harness and the cart should spend all their exercise sessions in both, and should be introduced to the physical rigours very gradually so that they will not be injured or soured mentally. Traditionally, jogging has practically always been done the 'wrong' way round, on the right rein, and fast work performed the 'right' way, on the left rein. Hence an older horse will often begin to catch hold and take interest when turned to the left. But some trainers maintain that it is bad form to work a young horse one way only, and do equal amounts on both reins to prevent him becoming 'one-sided'.

Most equestrians have their own pet methods of producing a horse hard and fit, and success is achieved along many avenues. To demonstrate this, two well respected trainers have kindly outlined their personal fittening programmes for this book as guidance to those unfamiliar with the kind of demands that are made on the harness racehorse.

Mick Yeomans has trained and driven many good winners, and this is the outline he has followed, working on a training track:

'Week 1 The horse will come straight from the field for me, and when he comes in I spend the initial week getting hard feed back into his digestive system. I use a cool-mix to begin with so as not to overdo it too quickly, and

Mick Yeomans, successful trainer and driver, leads the field with Stobart Express at Leominster.

worm him with a decent brand of wormer. He is shod with ordinary shoes suitable for basic jogging, and the first week is just allowing the horse to become accustomed to the exercise and the hard feed without being put under any strain or pressure.

Week 2 Steady jogging: 2 1/2 miles per day for six days. Sunday rest day.

Week 3 Steady jogging: 3 miles per day for six days. Sunday rest day.

Week 4 Steady jogging: 3 1/2 miles a day for six days. Sunday rest day.

Week 5 Steady jogging: 4 miles a day for six days. Sunday rest day.

Week 6 Steady jogging: 4 1/2 miles a day for six days. Sunday rest day.

Week 7 Steady jogging: 5 miles a day for six days. Sunday rest day.

Week 8 Steady jogging: 5 miles a day for six days. Sunday rest day.

Week 9 Steady jogging: 5 miles, Monday, Tuesday, Thursday and Friday. Wednesday: 2 miles jogging + 1 mile fast work at 2 minutes 50 seconds–3 minutes. Saturday: 2 miles jogging + 1 mile fast work at 2 minutes 50 seconds–3 minutes. Sunday, rest day.

Week 10 Steady jogging: 5 miles, Monday, Tuesday, Thursday and

Friday. Wednesday and Saturday: 2 miles jogging + 1 mile fast work at 2 minutes 40 seconds–2 minutes 50 seconds. Sunday, rest day.

Week 11 Steady jogging: 5 miles, Monday, Tuesday, Thursday and Friday. Wednesday and Saturday: fast work in heats. Heat 1: 1 mile at 2 minutes, 50 seconds. Half an hour later, heat 2: 1 mile at 2 minutes, 30 seconds. Sunday, rest day.

Week 12 Steady jogging: 5 miles, Monday, Tuesday, Thursday and Friday. Wednesday and Saturday: fast work in heats; heat 1: 1 mile at 2 minutes, 40 seconds. Half an hour later, heat 2: 1 mile at 2 minutes, 20 seconds. Sunday, rest day.

Week 13 Steady jogging: 5 miles, Monday, Tuesday, Thursday and Friday. Wednesday and Saturday: fast work in heats. Heat 1: 1 mile at 2 minutes, 30 seconds. Half an hour later, heat 2: 1 mile at 2 minutes, 20 seconds. Sunday, rest day.

'By following this training programme, the horse should have had enough conditioning work to enable him to qualify and last through a tough racing season.

'After the horse has recorded a qualifying time on the track, improvement should follow gradually, but keep the training programme as week 13, though perhaps the fast work heats could be five seconds faster each trip (i.e. heat 1: 2 minutes 25 seconds; heat 2: 2 minutes 15 seconds). Never work the horse within five seconds of his limit, leave the fast times for the races. When a horse is racing once a week, possibly on a Saturday, only one day of fast work will be required, for example on a Wednesday. Also, fast work heats can be reduced to one heat per work-out day, though this depends on the individual, and whether he is clean-winded or not. If racing more than once a week, this should be enough fast work and jogging between events should be sufficient. There must be a rest day each week. Turning a horse out in a grass paddock is an excellent way of keeping a horse sweet and in a good frame of mind.'

Public trainer, Dennis Hardwick, is a modest man who is highly successful. His brilliant stallion, Stoneriggs JR, is a prolific winner and top-class Free-for-All competitor. In 1991, JR had the distinction of taking both the Welsh Classic Free For All and the Welsh Classic Final at Tregaron.

Dennis has been involved with horses all his life. 'My first pony was bought in chapel on a Sunday night and cost £3.00. I rode that pony back and fore from school for several years. The little so-and-so was home before me on many a night!

'It was after I'd been to a harness racing meeting at Penybont that I decided to buy a pacer. I bought an unbroken five-year-old by Hang On, and most of my information on the job came from the late Mr Frank Bevan. I had a lot of fun and a few upsets with that horse. I then decided to join the British Harness Racing Club, and went up north to buy four horses. One of these was a bit of a pony, Stoneriggs JR!'

Dennis Hardwick lives in Wales, near Llandrindod Wells, and his training programme is fashioned to keep his horses fit in body and mind using the forestry, roads and fields that he has at hand.'If I intend to race in April, at the beginning of the season on grass, the horses will come into work on Boxing Day. After worming, each horse will do six weeks steady roadwork, normally under saddle. I think these first six weeks of building and strengthening muscles are probably the most important.

'After this, the horse will graduate to the cart, jogging quietly on the forestry roads for a further two weeks, without wearing hopples. After this

Dennis Hardwick's top class stallion, Stoneriggs JR, with Colin Bevan at Tregaron.

foundation work, I then start them in faster work in full kit and increase the feed according to the work. There is no point at all in training an underfed horse. If the horse starts to get sharp, I increase the work, but don't cut back on the feed. I keep increasing the distance on fast work until the horse can stay the distance of one and a quarter to one and a half miles. By then the horse should be able to stay the distance of one mile in a race.

'Remember never to chill a horse.

'The weekly routine for my horses following roadwork would be:

Sunday: Rest day.

Monday: 6–7 miles under saddle.

Tuesday: 6 miles in the cart.

Wednesday: Half an hour lungeing.

Thursday: 6–7 miles under saddle.

Friday: If racing following day, 2 miles walking.

Saturday: Race day; but, if not, 6–7 miles under saddle.

'I like to let my horses have an hour out in the field most days. When a horse is absolutely fit, I then rest him on Wednesday as well as Sunday, cutting out the lungeing. It is terribly tempting to overwork a fit horse. Four basic points for success are: a good horse, good feed, a good farrier and lots of commonsense from both the horse and the trainer!'

Both these programmes have produced plenty of winners and lots of pleasure for owners. And, as Dennis says, commonsense needs to be liberally applied, though perhaps commonsense is not so common. Of course, there are many other different programmes, and those involved with interval-training for other disciplines would do well to adapt the methods to apply to harness racing. Some trainers swim lazy horses to put an edge on fitness, but, just as in Thoroughbred racing, you either believe in it or you don't. Stevie Lees is of the opinion that it would only be of use if you were training horses for swimming races, but many trainers do use the pool to vary routine or if a horse has a slight leg injury which would incapacitate it for normal exercise.

It is almost impossible to advise a set feeding programme to complement the work of a harness racehorse, since this is something that must be unique to the individual. No two horses could be fed the same, as requirements vary so very much from horse to horse, so it is best only to include a few basic rules. The first of these is that anything fed *must* be of top-class

Some trainers swim their charges to put an edge on fitness or if they suffer slight leg injuries.

quality. There is an old saying, 'Bad hay is not even good litter,' and this is but a mild observation. The harsh truth is that the spores in suspect hay (it doesn't even have to *look* mouldy) can cause havoc to the respiratory system, at best causing your horse to run like a big hairy dog instead of a racehorse, and at worst can result in broken windedness.

Every trainer has his own beliefs regarding whether to feed a complete mix, oats or cubes, or maybe a combination of these. The compound feeds are useful, because they are nutritionally balanced with the correct ratio of vitamins and minerals, eliminating the need for additives. Once a horse begins serious work, he must graduate to those with a higher protein content, designed for high-performance horses. Any change in feed must not be made suddenly, or the digestive system will become upset and the horse will lose condition at a crucial time. Oats are an old favourite, and are best if bought direct from the farm, ideally being just 'bruised' or 'cracked' through a roller. This process should not be done too far in advance, or valuable goodness will be lost. Nowadays, an oat balancer is available as an efficient additive to provide some of the nutrients that may otherwise be lacking from a diet of grain. The majority of equestrians tend to use too many additives, often doubling up on minerals, etc., as they are swayed by 'fads' created by imaginative marketing on behalf of the manufacturers. As vitamins cannot be stored in the body, this is a shocking waste of money that ends up on the muckheap without having done an ounce of good on the way! Check all the labels on whatever feedstuffs and additives you use to make sure that you are not guilty.

The hard and fast rules of feeding racehorses are 'feed according to work', and 'little and often'. Basically, if a horse is working hard, give him as much as he will eat in four feeds over 24 hours, having increased his ration as his work gets faster. You will need really to get to know your horse, and it is better to keep him looking for the feed rather than overface him, or risking him 'tying up' painfully with azoturia, often caused by too much feed and too little work, though there are unfortunately some horses who are just prone to it. There have even been cases of laminitis in Thoroughbreds from over-zealous feeding of high protein feeds. So you can see why feeding is a science: feed too much and you will create problems, feed too little and your horse will be unable to do himself justice. Finicky feeders are a real challenge, for they must be tempted to the manger or they will be unable to cope with the demands of training. Golden Dale is very choosy about what he eats, and Clifford Haythornthwaite, his trainer, has given up trying to insist on what he *should* eat, but makes sure that what does take his fancy is the best available.

Molasses are useful for damping feed (which is vital), and horses love them once they are used to them. Some prefer a handful of well soaked sugar beet with their oats. Grated apple and carrots carefully incorporated in the feed so the horse cannot just pick them out are also a good ploy. The usual invention of knocking a small hole in the wall so that he can see the next horse at his manger also works as well as ever it did. And a turnout paddock is a wonderful tonic. So long as it is not lush grass that a horse can 'pig' himself on, he will be happier and healthier out for a couple of hours, and some horses will eat better if fed in the field (alone, though, or a kicking match will ensue).

Weigh a scoop of feed now and again to make sure you know exactly how much you are feeding, and remember that different substances vary in weight; for example, if your level scoop of oats weighs 3 lb, the same scoop of nuts will be heavier.

As a very rough guide, a 15 hh Standardbred in strong work who is of a normal disposition (i.e. not the hyperactive, nervy type) should perform on 12–14 lb of hard feed a day, in addition to hay, and the bigger animals, if they are not the 'stuffy', thick-winded sort, might need between 15–18 lb a day. But there are big horses who need a lot less and small horses who eat a lot more; feeding has to be played very much by ear, with an eye kept constantly on condition and well-being. An underfed horse will not cope with the rigours of physical stress, and will find staying the 'trip' (distance of a race) difficult.

Electrolytes are very important, and replace all the body salts, etc., that are lost by sweating. They should *always* be given after racing or working out, particularly on a hot day, and a horse that sweats easily may need them daily in his race build-up and recovery. If possible, try to encourage a horse to imbibe them when he is offered water following a race, particularly if he has a run in a final to follow. But ensure that he happily accepts them as a matter of routine before doing this, and do not risk him refusing water at the races, which may lead to dehydration. A simple test to 'diagnose' suspected dehydration is to pick a small section of skin on the horse's neck or shoulder between finger and thumb and just pull it gently away from the body. If it is slack and unelastic, not returning to position immediately, he indeed needs fluids desperately.

Clean water should be always available in the stable, except for the obvious times such as just before or after a race or fast workout, and careful note should be taken of how much water the horse drinks, as this is also a positive indication of his well-being. A normal horse may imbibe between 8–10 gallons a day, and needs this amount to keep his kidneys flushed and his system operating efficiently. Automatic drinkers obviously save on the labour of hauling buckets of water about, but they won't tell you if a horse is drinking normally. A horse that has free access to water rarely drinks at unsuitable moments, like after a full feed, and it is unnatural to insist that he drinks at certain times. If he is the annoying type of colt who enjoys tipping his bucket and breaking it to create entertainment for himself (this is where turning out helps to alleviate such boredom), use a heavier, metal container and give him 'toys' to play with, a football usually being a favourite. However, a supply of these is necessary for the colt hellbent on destruction. Standing the bucket in an old tyre is not a sound idea for this sort, as he will probably drag it into the middle of his box, and may injure his legs. As Aberystwyth trainer, Peter Davies, rightly points out, it is impossible to take a rigid programme of either feeding or training and apply it religiously to any horse. A programme has to be treated as a framework within which to operate, and the guidelines must be altered according the requirements of that particular animal.

Most trainers use a stopwatch to gauge a horse's performance in fast work, and, certainly on the hard tracks, it is a vital asset. On the much slower grass surface, it is much more difficult to apply time to performance since grass circuits vary considerably. Judgement of pace then becomes the all-important factor, and this is one of the talents that makes a driver top class.

During fast work, a horse's action should be closely observed, so that shoeing and correction of the foot can be applied to obtain maximum performance on the track. As in all performance horses, a blood test from the vet will help to pinpoint any problems, and a cell count is very helpful in knowing exactly how fit your horse is. Bedding is also important for producing a fit horse: straw is nowadays undesirable, because chemical sprays are used on the standing wheat and they cause irritation in the respiratory tract. Most horses will pick at straw and become either bulky or colicky, even when it is doused with disinfectant. Though this is often practised, is not recommended, since spores breed in damp straw and cause yet more irritation in the lungs. Shavings appear to be the most popular bedding used by the harness racing fraternity, but even they can be dusty unless the best, most expensive quality bales are purchased. Shredded paper is certainly the best for any horses who suffer with wind or sinus problems, and it is much more economical than shavings. Some trainers complain that it is messy on the muckheap, but this drawback is outweighed by the advantage of it being dust-free.

For the new driver, it is essential to get behind a horse at every opportunity, and preferably as many different horses as possible, to widen your experience and prevent yourself having what Gwyne Higgins derides as 'one pair of hands for one type of horse'. All horses are individuals, and you cannot rigidly adhere to a programme without taking this into account. There are some horses which are so stuffy they have to actually have a pipe-opener before they leave for the races, and some which need nothing more than an hour in the field daily between weekly races. Training gives the opportunity of getting to know your horse completely, which will automatically give you confidence on the sulky seat at the races.

Occasionally you hear people talk about 'racing a horse fit' but running a horse who is not fit and well is asking for an injury (tired muscles strain easily); nor is it recommended for his mental state. A clever horse who thinks that a race is going to hurt is not going to be too keen to give it his best shot even when he is fit, if he has achieved that state by constantly going through a pain-barrier under pressure.

One of the attractions of harness racing is that a broad spectrum of people enjoy driving. Thus there are architects, clerks, builders and all sorts out there amongst the professionals. And though driving is not as physically demanding as riding in a race, the driver with a sedentary occupation should not neglect a fitness programme for himself or he will be blowing louder than the horse after the race, and his muscles will complain so loudly that he will only be able to hobble carefully off the sulky the first couple of times! Any physical exercise will help, particularly skipping sessions, but it is another reason to be on the sulky for the home workouts.

With all the tribulations of training horses, perhaps yoga or some other form of mental relaxation would be advisable. Failing that, fit a very strong lock on the drinks cabinet!

5

At the Races

Due to the inherent toughness of the breed, it is much easier to keep a Standardbred in one piece during his preparation for racing than a Thoroughbred racehorse. There are of course exceptions – Ian Drysdale comments that training horses is 'months of agony for moments of pleasure'. His own patience paid dividends when Helen Sinclair's Johnny's Decision won the Centenary Famous Musselburgh Pace after being off the track for two years with leg problems.

As with all racehorses, it is well to remember that it is far simpler to overtrain a horse than undertrain it; it's all too easy to leave your race at home. But now, with all those miles of jogging behind you, the goal which you have worked towards is at hand – a day at the races!

Entries have to be made at least a week in advance in writing to the appropriate secretary. (If you are racing on a hard track, a list of secretaries is available from BHRC. If you are racing on grass, a list of secretaries will be available from the promoter of that region, for example Eden Valley or Wales and the West (see pp.106–7). It is advisable to become a member of your local 'body', because this not only entitles you to a vote in the local issues, but will keep you informed of what's going on). All regions run championships, which often include 'Best Novice Driver' or 'Best Newcomer' and unless a member of that particular association, you will be ineligible.

Unlike point-to-pointing, the organizers don't usually expect the fee to accompany the entry, though the major meetings like a deposit through the post. (These usually have special entry forms with the conditions printed on them which are sent out with the *Calendar*. Entries also often close earlier than normal, so look closely.) The debt is generally settled when 'declaring' (announcing you are present and stating your inten-

Mrs Helen Sinclair's Johnny's Decision, winning the centenary Famous Musselburgh Pace with George Drysdale after two years off the track.

tion to run your horse, naming your driver) with the secretary on the day, and collecting your number cloth. If you do not actually run your horse on the day, yet have not withdrawn your horse within the stipulated time (usually two days prior to the meeting) you will be expected to supply the full entry fee. Entries used to be accepted over the 'phone for all meetings, causing monumental headaches for secretaries when owners could not remember various details about their horses, and now everyone is encouraged to quote the horse's passport number and the licence registration number of the driver. This helps Weatherby's sort t'other from which, for in the past the profusion of Wilsons, Lees, etc., without identification have probably had the computer on the brink of self-detonation.

Most secretaries are highly efficient, and the handicap sheets containing the runners in their allocated races for a Saturday fixture usually drop onto the doormats before mid-week. Then you know what you are up against. Also, unlike point-to-pointing, most horses that are entered for a race actually run, unless they suffer a setback, so generally, what you see on the handicap sheet is what you get. This is where the race begins for you, because the opposition must be thoroughly studied, and, if possible, by dint of asking around or studying form, you must try to become acquainted with the best time each runner is capable of achieving in a race, and compare it with the ability of your own horse. Champion driver, Mike Lord, points out that the object of racing is to *win*, and the experience gained from the test drives should be enough for a new driver to go out and be able to do just that, providing he has the horsepower.

Mike explains, 'It's essential that you know your horse. From working

If you can hold your position on the inner, the opposition has to come wide. Here Tiffany holds pole position on the bend at Wreningham.

at home you should know the time he can do over a mile, and the time he does over each quarter of the race to achieve it. The first and last quarters are especially important. You need to know the time he can sprint home in the last quarter; for instance, some horses can only sprint at top speed for the maximum of three hundred yards, so there would be no use setting him alight four hundred yards out, would there? Some horses cannot sprint early *and* late in a race, so if you have one of those, you have to beware of burning him out sprinting for position early on. It is vitally important to formulate a race-plan, and to be utterly decisive in a race. The decisions you make must be *safe*, and you must commit yourself to them. If you are getting behind a horse you don't know, you must ask the trainer about him. You need input to know how to drive him to the best of his ability. Does he like to front-run, or does he like a 'tow' from a horse in front of him? Some horses idle unless they have a horse upsides (beside) them. Being a good driver is not just about winning on the best horse, it's about winning races with those that aren't necessarily the best, which is where race tactics come into it. Study the card and get to know about the other horses, that's crucial. And because it's more or less impossible for me to store the information about ten horses in my brain, I discard those that I consider have no chance, and concentrate on those I think will be the dangers.' So thinking about the race begins in earnest several days (and probably nights, if you are of sensitive temperament) before.

Once horses begin regular fast work, they are usually shod with the shoes they will race in, the light aluminium plates or the lightweight pacing shoes, or a mixture of the two, whatever the individual horse requires. This is best achieved by someone who knows the horse, or a farrier who is well acquainted with the sport. In fact there are quite a few of them who train and drive themselves – Gary Wakefield, Mike Strickland, Evelyn Slack and Geoff Meachin included – but race day is one of their days off, and none would be overjoyed at the prospect of having to plate a horse up at a meeting! So the shoes should be sorted well in advance, so that you can judge whether there is an improvement to be made. The grass nails, used to help a horse grip on the track surface, are not applied until the day before or the morning of a meeting. These are nails with a large head which protrude just enough to give a small amount of traction and assist a horse in keeping his footing on the bends. The farrier will replace a few of the normal nails with these in each foot, but it does not take long for them to become worn down and their usefulness reduced. Again, depending on the action of the particular horse, some people use a small stud in the outside of each hind shoe for improved grip, but these should only be screwed in prior to working out on race day. If you intend to use them, don't forget to ask the farrier to stamp a stud hole in the shoe when the horse is being shod, and each hole is best packed with *oiled* cotton wool if you don't wish to be fiddling endlessly with stud taps to clean it out when you should be tacking up at the races. Most harness racing people own a farrier's hammer with which to implement emergency repairs to 'sprung' (misshapen) plates, etc., and it is certainly a wise investment.

As with any discipline, it is best to have a hamper or trunk that is packed with the general items you need around performance horses. These include all the veterinary paraphernalia, grooming and washing-down tack, spares, etc. Apart from the harness, driver's colours, white trousers, skull cap, body protector, gadgets and obvious equipment, other vital components of a stress-free day include all BHRC licences and passports (the latter must include the record of 'flu jabs which must comply with BHRC/Jockey Club regulations) which should be available for inspection at all times, a couple of bungee clips for attaching number cloths, a footpump for soft tyres, all the relevant spanners for replacing wheels, seats, etc., a few pieces of baler twine which always comes in useful for something, and the inevitable stopwatch. As with most horse events, it is usually best to transport your own water, as there is rarely any on hand, and don't underestimate your needs, especially if it's a filthy wet day.

So, armed with directions from the secretary if you are not familiar with the venue (sadly, most tracks are not overblessed with signs), and having remembered to include the cart in the luggage (some people have been known to forget to hang it on the back when they have got in a rush!) you can set sail with hope in your heart, in plenty of time. For a 2 p.m. start, most people will have arrived long before midday, and if you have not declared by one o'clock, you will probably not be included in the draw for positions and automatically be placed on the outside (the worst position). Once you arrive at the circuit and have checked on your horse, it is best to get the declarations done at the secretary's office and collect the number cloth, checking that the one you are given corresponds with that on the racecard, and that all details on it relating to your entry are correct.

It is an offence to work out on the track without the appropriate number cloth, and all drivers must be correctly attired in their colours, white trousers and skull caps. Some raceways now ban drivers wearing training shoes or similar whilst driving, so it is best to stick to jodhpur boots, which also prevent the footrests rubbing and causing blisters.

Jock Ritchie Jnr (Cult Remarkable) and Robert Wilson (Candy Penash) clashed wheels at Errol and this was the result! All walked away unscathed.

Though most people jog at home with a headcollar under the horse's bridle, this is definitely *not* allowed at the races and a quick ticket to a fine from the stewards. So using a headcollar which can unbuckle at the noseband as well as the headpiece is extremely helpful, so that it can be slipped off when the tacking up is completed. Working out is usually done on the track, provided conditions are not excessively wet, in which case it will be announced. Sometimes the inside 'lane' is coned off to save it deteriorating, so just keep your eye on what the stewards are indicating. And keep your wits about you! The unwritten law is that the fast sprints are practised on the inside, so if you are warming up or down slowly, stay two or three wide and watch out for those behind you. When you go up a gear or two, depending on what warm-up your particular horse needs, move onto the inside. It is advisable never to pull up and come off the track straight away at the exit, but turn and come back a long way past it, keeping to the right, so that your horse never gets the idea of napping to come off there.

You should have time to have worked out and cooled off your horse

Steve Flook and Vrnwy Joker return relatively unscathed following a fall at Allensmore. Beaten but unbowed!

before the draw is made. It isn't essential to be there, but many drivers like to know where they are going to be in advance, so that they may adapt their tactics accordingly. To be drawn one off the starting gate is the 'pole' position on the inside. Number two draw is the next position, on the outside of one, and up to draw five (or sometimes seven, depending on the track) are still just behind the start car, becoming accordingly more to the outside. If all runners are off level handicaps (for example in maiden races where all horses are eligible to start directly behind the gate) draw numbers above this are off the 'second line' directly behind the front one, with the lower numbers working from the inside positions outwards. Obviously, the inside draw (1) is the most desirable, since mathematicians have calculated that a horse pacing five feet from the inside marker will travel 62 feet farther than the horse on the inside over a mile on a half-mile circuit. Anyone drawn on the outside who wishes to dictate the pace obviously has to use early speed to get to the front. Once past the starting post, it is up to the driver to choose position, and most move inwards. There are strict rules regarding dangerous driving, and anyone overtaking must allow ten feet clearance before cutting in towards the inside in front of the horse that has been passed. Obviously, it is much further for a horse to have to race on the outside, and a horse that tucks in behind the leader on the inside gets some 'cover', minimizing the wind resistance. The draw for position is often crucial to the result; at certain tracks where the bends come quickly and the company is 'hot', an outside draw will diminish a horse's chance of winning. If possible, until you have driven a race or two, try to take note of who is drawn on each side of you, it will help you to find position behind the gate, and you can gauge who you think is likely to try and lead, and what their tactics will be.

Depending on the safety factor (number of runners allowed) of the track (this varies considerably from track to track, but is generally about ten starters) sometimes the novice grades are split into more than one race on the day if entries exceed this and all declare. Either way, there are plenty of races to get through, and the organizers do not hang about between them. Sometimes a meeting will stipulate a break of twenty minutes or so between each event to give the busy drivers time to draw breath, but at many fixtures, the prizewinners will be leaving the track as the runners for the next are coming out to parade, so be on the ball. Before you get on the cart to warm up quietly just before a race, always cast a weather-eye over the harness, just to make sure all is in order. 'But the most important things to check,' advises Mike Lord, 'are that the reins are buckled onto the bit securely, and that your front hopple carrier straps are threaded right through the buckle attaching the hopple. It's not enough for the pin just to be in the hole, the rest of the strap must be through the buckle or there may be a chance of the pin getting flicked out. If the back ones come undone, it's no picnic, and you'll have to pull up, but if the front ones come adrift, it's odds-on that you'll end up on the deck at speed. So no matter how rushed you are, get into the habit of *always* checking those two things.'

At some raceways and major meetings on grass, there will be a paddock in which you will be required to parade prior to appearing on the track. There will be a steward breathing fire here to ensure that no-one is late (another fineable offence) and will sort the runners into race card order for the benefit of the crowd.

The official starter will generally confirm every runner's draw position and handicap (the latter having been automatically allotted at the time of entry by Weatherbys) so that there will be no confusion at the start. A horse that has won one race will have a handicap of 10 yards (termed 'class 010') and will start 10 yards behind the gate (start car); two victories would mean he would start 20 yards (class 020) behind the gate and so on, to a maximum penalty of 80 yards (class 080). In practice this means as the 'gate' (class 000) horses are passing the starting post, the runners handicapped off 80 yards will be 80 yards behind. Naturally, the race timing begins as the front horses cross the starting line, so if an 80-yard horse then wins in 2 minutes 10 seconds, he has actually covered 1 mile, 80 yards in that time, so his mile rate would be considerably faster than the actual race time. The official calculation is that a horse covers 12 yards a second, though of course much depends on the track surface and going conditions, so the 80-yard horse winning in 2.10 would actually have paced the mile in 2.3.5 (2 minutes, 3.5 seconds).

The driver's feet must remain in the footrests at *all* times when driving on the track, and any contravention of this rule means an instant fine. Reins dragging and loose number cloths are other illegalities, as is speaking to anyone other than a judge or steward, so explain to your adoring family beforehand that they must not be upset by your lack of communication.

When the crowd has had reasonable time to inspect the runners, the start car will cruise quietly to the opposite side of the track, where the horses will be expected to join it in somewhere near their correct positions. It is here that even the quietest horses can take a fierce grip or do something uncharacteristic as the adrenalin begins to flow. The gate will gather speed, and most start-car drivers are expert at calculating the pace. But it is at this juncture that things can go wrong. Conway Price, who was official starter in Wales and the West, developed nerves of steel as tonnes of hurtling horseflesh misbehaved behind the gate, though any horse that consistently does so can either be ordered to requalify or be placed on the outside. Welsh driver, Paul Evans, renowned for his fast getaways, can claim to be one of the few to have 'limboed' under a starting gate when Raceover Jack took a serious hold in an International Invitation Race at Tir Prince Raceway and sprinted past the gate, with Paul horizontal on the sulky to avoid being decapitated by the 'wing'! Dilly's Springtime unseated Sandy Cassells at the start of a novice race at Corbiewood Stadium and ran loose around the track for at least three miles, before being recaptured. Despite her escapade, the filly cruised

'I surrender'. Conway Price, official starter, developed nerves of steel as tons of horseflesh hurtled behind the gate.

home to win comfortably. So there are occasionally incidents, though most races get away without problem – but watch yourself! Make no mistake, anything involving horses at speed is a dangerous pastime, and when any mishap occurs in a race, everything usually happens too quickly for any evasive action.

Ensure that you don't drive too closely to the inner rail or markers, which will flip you over if you hit one. And if you don't allow the ten feet clearance and cut in too quickly when overtaking, the horse behind will strike your sulky with his forelegs and probably trip. Similarly, trying to get through a gap that is not wide enough will bring a horse down and cause chaos, because those travelling behind will not be able to avoid the confusion. If 'parked' on the outside, hold your horse off the one on your inside, because your horse will probably tend to lean inwards, especially on the bends, and may force the horse on your inner into the inside rail, or, at the very least, cause a clash of wheels which may 'deck' you both.

OVERLEAF *Some of the top horses in 1993 contest a Free-for-All at Tir Prince.* (Left to right) *UK record-holder, Golden Dale (Alan Haythornthwaite), Saunders Destiny (Mike Lord), Stoneriggs JR (Colin Bevan) and Nijinsky (Mike Stutter).*

The stewards take a very dim view of dangerous driving, and if they are dissatisfied with the performance of an individual they are empowered to insist that he re-take a driving test. Any fines incurred on a race day are required to be settled before the perpetrator leaves the meeting.

The starter will shout instructions from his 'platform' on the car, and needless to say he must be obeyed. When the green light flashes, he will probably yell, 'Look after yourselves!' which is the best advice anyone can give in a race!

Keeping hold of your horse's head is most important in a race, and, though you are obviously out to do your best, top driver, Alan Haythornthwaite, believes that new drivers shouldn't be too ambitious on their first couple of runs. 'It will all go really quickly the first few times. I think that it's a good thing to learn to sit still and keep the horse balanced, take time to look around you and see what's going on in a race. You're bound to be tense, so try to relax and think clearly. But it really is vitally important that a new driver has had lots of experience working out at home so that he does things naturally, and if things do go wrong, he reacts by reflex, not by having to think about it.' Alan agrees with Mike Lord that a driver should have done his homework and know approximately what each horse is likely to do in a race, or if any have a habit of breaking, for instance. 'But nothing is ever black and white, and I find it difficult to drive to a plan. Some horses may improve according to the track or the going, or some drivers may try different tactics with a horse. This may be due to the previous ones not working, or perhaps to confuse the opposition! Golden Dale (who holds three UK records) used to go out in front to make the pace, then just when the other drivers thought they knew how he was likely to run in a race, I tucked him in and came from behind! The fact that I could vary his running like that was one of his greatest strengths.

'Basically, you should be travelling as quickly as you can, without being in top gear. The best way to describe this is to imagine that you have a car with only a gallon of petrol in it to get from A to B. You have to utilize that petrol to get that distance as well as you can, whether it's going fast then steady, steady then fast, or steady all the way. That depends on your horse. But you've only got that gallon in the tank, and once that's gone, there's no more performance. Joe Sowerby, who's a very shrewd trainer, told me that years ago when I first started, and Michael Dickinson, who was so successful as a National Hunt trainer, apparently used to tell his young jockeys the same thing.'

Both Alan and Mike agree that experience is the key. 'The difference between the top flight drivers and the others is that the top drivers make

Making a forward move creates 'holes' and the horse on the inner finds a gap. Stoneriggs Glory (Roy Wilson) goes for home as Charmagres Gold (Gary Wakefield) shades Stoneriggs Herbie (the author).

more right decisions than wrong ones. It's only experience that brings that,' observed Mike. Alan, ever realistic, added, 'But no-one can be right all the time!'

Mike enlarged on the importance that tactics play in a race. 'Say you have a horse that is capable of recording 2.10 over the mile and he's drawn one off the car (start car). If your horse will front run (lead), then use the advantage to get to the front and dictate the pace. The horse that you know can do 2.9 and is the greatest danger is now behind you, and he's going to have to come wide to get by you. If you can, get your brain in gear and use the other runners as obstacles, because if you know that your horse can travel his last quarter in 31 seconds, the opposition, in order to come three or four wide round the outside and beat you, is going to have to step out in 29 seconds. If something comes upsides you, don't panic, especially if it isn't one of the horses you had earmarked as a danger. He not only has to get by you, he has to be ten feet clear of you, but you don't really want to increase your pace because you're trying to conserve energy for the last quarter. Try to just hold that horse on your outside into the bends, which means he'll be on your wheel in the straights. So that danger horse is going to have to use precious energy by coming at you three wide (around three horses). If that's where he is in the final quarter, go for it, because he's going to have to go faster than the 31 seconds you know your horse can do to get by you, and if you don't move then, you'll lose the advantage. But if he's on the inner behind you, don't make your move, because if you go for it, it creates 'holes' (gaps) and he'll find the space to run and challenge you. Keep him behind you as long as you can, and when he makes his run, he'll have to come round a wall of horses.

'Similarly, if there is a good horse upsides you at the half pole (halfway marker) that has come off a thirty or forty yard trail and the race has gone in 1.2 (1 minute, 2 seconds) at that stage, you can forget him, he's not going to get home because he has used too much energy to get to that position at that speed. But if that same horse is upsides you and the race has gone in 1.5, you're going to have to start thinking seriously of ways to make him use himself, or accept that you're probably going to get beat!'

This acceptance is not something that Mike Lord is familiar with, and this straightforward advice illustrates how devious the racing brain has to be. 'Cunning' is probably one of the greatest compliments that can be paid to a driver.

There are a few regulations concerning the whip. The instrument itself should not exceed four feet in length, with a 'snapper' no longer than eight inches. There is also a rule which requires drivers to keep both hands on the reins during a race, which, in theory, ought to prevent whip abuse (which is another heftily punishable offence). But Alan advocates that novice drivers are better off not using the whip anyway. 'Most would only unbalance a horse. And usually, it's only lazy horses that need that sort of encouragement. Any horse that's doing its best and gets striped for it is more likely to think, "Blow this!" and stop rather than run.'

Though Alan Haythornthwaite is a true professional and winning races is his bread and butter, he stresses that nothing is worth doing unless it is enjoyable, so wherever you finish in your first race 'proper', savour the sensations of speed and power, and the fact that you are a part of the heart-fluttering action. Gary Wakefield once said that he'd drive in the Famous Musselburgh Pace if the prize money was only five pounds, never mind five thousand. And, though Alan gaily misquoted, 'It isn't the taking part, it's the winning that counts!' most drivers would rather be out there with an also-ran than watching from the sidelines. Mike put it into perspective. 'I'm lucky enough to earn my living doing something I like. If I didn't, I'd have to have a job that earned me the money to be able to go harness racing!'

6

The Breaking Process

The basics of educating a harness horse are much the same as educating any other in the early stages, but then it gets trickier. Unless you are either well versed in the art, or the kind of strange character who enjoys collecting interesting bruises, breaking is best left to the experts.

Many trainers will expect to race the animal for whom they risk life, limb and sexual inadequacy when instilling the basics, though some are perfectly happy to perform the breaking process, and then pack the youngster off home to owners who will hopefully have the knowledge to continue handling and training him. Again, ask around if you wish to pursue the latter course, and discover who is recommended. As Arthur Slack, master of the renowned Stoneriggs Stud, wisely observes, 'A lot of men have horses, but very few are horsemen.'

This early formative training is vital as a grounding throughout a horse's life, whatever his career, so don't expect it to happen in five minutes. Anyone who reckons they can have your youngster in the cart and driving in a week is a cowboy, and has cut vital corners, even if the horse is of a placid temperament. Just imagine driving an excited horse who does not respond to the reins due to having 'no mouth' in a bunch of others and you will *know* that it is worth spending money at this stage to have the thing done properly. And you often hear people from all branches of equestrianism talk about 're-breaking' an unmannered horse, but, sadly, it is difficult to eradicate bad habits that have been learned where he should have been taught good ones; horses are blessed with terrific memories, the trick is to make sure they remember what they are supposed to. To make sure the youngster does not acquire any evasions, by accident or design, there should always be two people to implement most stages of breaking the young horse.

Obviously, the more a horse can be handled as a foal and in his first year, the easier he should be (in theory) to break. The only exception to this would be if he happens to be a cheeky individual, and he is allowed to become over-confident to the point where he does not respect his handler, who has been too timid to put him in his place. A recipe for disaster, since a battle will be unavoidable sooner or later. Like children, horses should be made aware of right and wrong from the outset, with praise for the former and swift, sharp retribution for the latter. Also, though youngsters need adequate nutrition to ensure that they mature to their full potential, don't make the mistake of overdoing it, for, though most equestrians are unaware of it, irreparable damage can be done to immature bones through Degenerative Joint Disease (DJD), which is often caused in young horses by over-zealous feeding and stimulated by excess intake of vitamins and minerals. Gloucestershire veterinary surgeon, Brendan Paterson, explains, 'Foals are produced, particularly in the Thoroughbred industry, with the genetic blueprint that ensures that they grow quickly to become large and well grown yearlings. Obviously DJD is a multi-factored complaint, but certainly an energy-dense diet and the resulting demands on skeletally immature animals contribute heavily towards the alarming increase in this disease. Often the owner is unaware of the problem, since the horse does not usually become acutely lame, more stiff, particularly when the stifle joints are affected.'

DJD affects the developing cartilage within a joint and is synonymous with arthritis unless diagnosed and treated in the early stages. Ulcerated flap-like lesions or bone-cysts form on load-bearing, immature joints. These are difficult to detect with X-rays alone, and a surgical procedure with an arthroscope is often employed. The prognosis is poor for advanced cases. And all this before the horse is even broken! So recall the phrase 'killing with kindness' when delving into the feed-bin for your youngster, and, at the very least, bear in mind the difficulties of trying to educate a creature who is bursting with energy and as batty as an owl due to being full of corn.

Russell Andrew, based in Cardiff, is well known for the success of his 'Leckwith'-prefixed horses. Leckwith Pride held the UK two-year-old mile record with Gary Wakefield for three years, and Leckwith Gipsy was one of the leading horses in the 1993 season, winning nine races with Terry Laventure, including the Welsh Classic Three-Year-Old Championship at Tregaron in the fastest time of the meeting. Russell breeds and produces his own horses for the track, and Terry Laventure, who partners them, mostly breaks them as yearlings.

'The youngsters are all taught to be led in their first week,' explained Terry. 'They spend the summer out with their mothers, but are often brought in to have their feet trimmed. So they are used to being handled when they come in as yearlings in the autumn. The first thing I do then is put a rug on them, so they become used to having something put on and taken off them.' In the winter of 1993, Terry and Russell had eight yearlings to educate. Some of these would hopefully be forward enough to contest the two-year-old Classics, the Futurities and the Sires Stakes, but some may be broken, and then given time to mature.

'We mess with a yearling's legs as much as possible, and the breaking begins in earnest by putting on a bridle and mouthing bit with keys that he can play with. We always use an open bridle to begin with, I can never understand people who put blinkers on from the start, a horse might injure himself on the doorway of the stable, and wouldn't be able to see you when being lunged and get confused. We just leave the bridle on in the stable to begin with. The bit shouldn't be too tight so that it rubs the corner of the mouth, nor too loose so that he gets his tongue over, which is a bad habit that's difficult to shift.

'The pad and crupper are the next things we introduce and he can roam around the box with them on for three days to a week, depending on the individual. I know that some horses can go a bit crazy when you put the pad on for the first time, but all ours are so used to having the rug on that it isn't a problem. However, it's best not to pull up the girth tightly straight away, let them feel it for a few minutes first. But they're all different temperaments, and I can tell by the reaction of each one whether he is nervy and

Elasticated side-reins and hopple-hangers are introduced.

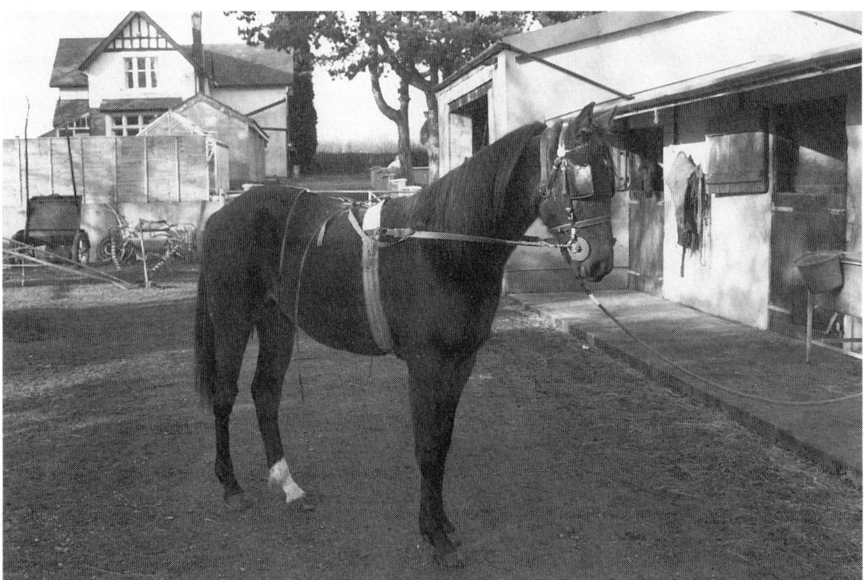

Terry line-driving (long-reining) the colt. He does this for at least a week 'to put a mouth' on the youngster.

will want more time over a particular stage. We lunge every day with the tack on, using a cavesson, never straight off the bit. When I think the horse is ready, I put sidelines on for a couple of hours, a couple of elasticated side-reins running from the pad to the bit to get him used to having to answer to the feel of the bit. At first I usually run a cord loosely from the bit rings through the ring that the overcheck fastens to on the pad just to stop him dropping his head between his knees and evading the bit. The sidelines are put on very loosely to begin with, then tightened gradually. If a horse is happy and relaxed with everything, and answering to the bit, I usually move on to long reining, with the long reins through the tugs. We just do it quietly, with one of us leading him off round the track, with the other walking behind. Depending on the temperament of the horse, I long-rein for at least a week, getting him used to turning left and right, and standing still. I use my voice a lot so that he gets to know vocal commands, and the tone of my voice and what it means.' Making sure that a horse knows what is required of him is half the battle. Some hiccups are caused solely because he is confused, and Terry does his utmost to prevent any communication breakdown.

Getting a horse accustomed to the hopples is the next step. 'I let the hangers just dangle for quite a time before I actually start using the hopples, and sometimes I put chains on them as an introduction. I usually just walk a horse round the stable with the hopples on to begin with, or if they're nervy, like Leckwith Tom, I strip them down and just put the back ones on. It's just a case of knowing how ready and confident a horse is. The overcheck is usually introduced at this time in the stable too, just hooked up very loosely, and tightened gradually every day. Some will fight it, and this is a good time to get the teeth checked, because wolf teeth seem to be aggravated by the check bit. It's best to try and eliminate problems before they actually occur. You should always notice how they are carrying their heads, that gives a clue as to whether anything else is wrong, not only teeth, but the back as well.'

Terry is a naturally quiet person, and likes to break his charges with the minimum of fuss. 'Some people like to bang and crash and frighten a horse half to death "to get him used to it", but that isn't my way. And some people like to get them dragging tractor tyres about before they put the cart on, but I don't rate that either. The horse is tied up to an outside wall every day to be mucked out, and harnessed up, and it's most important that he learns to stand quietly. When we consider that he is ready for the cart, we tie him to the wall and let him see it, and sniff it if he wants to, then, if he's OK, we just

Terry often pads the shafts to prevent them chafing a youngster.

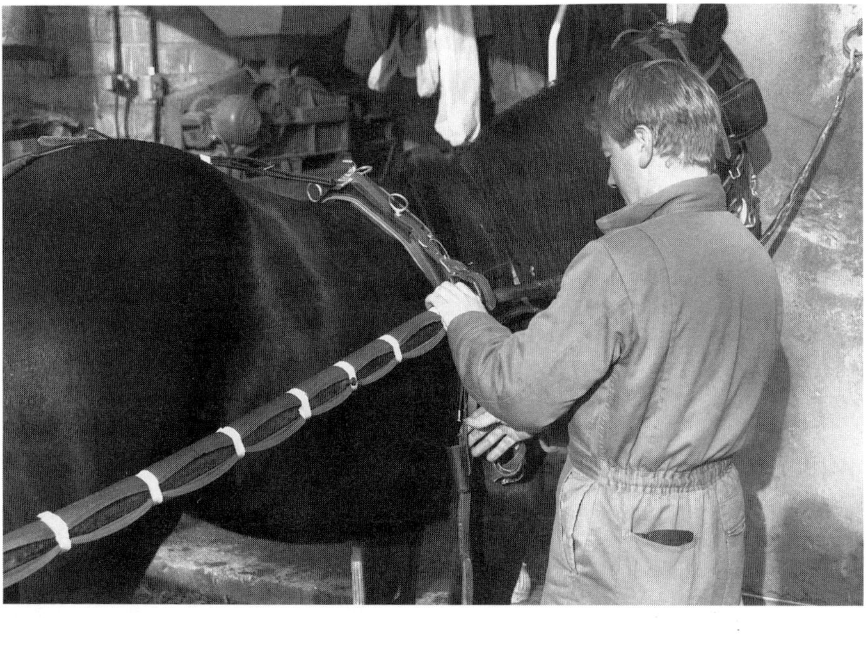

The blinkers prevent the youngster from being alarmed by the sulky behind him.

thread the shafts through the tugs and let him feel them, hoping that he doesn't climb the wall! Some do, of course, but some accept it, and, if all is well, we lead him off just like that, really quietly without the shafts attached properly. On the second day, we hook up the traces. I might put padding on the shafts for some of them, but we don't use a cart with extended shafts or a kick bar across. If they look like being a problem in that department, I just fix a kicking strap from one shaft to the other firmly across his back just in front of the hindquarters. This prevents him 'rising' to kick. We spend a long time leading and driving with the sulky behind, giving the same commands that he is used to. He usually walks about a mile with the cart on at first on the track, going on both reins, which is quite enough for a baby. Gradually I sit on the seat and see what the reaction is and take it from there. I mostly put blinkers on when we get to the cart stage, and once the horse is happily being driven from the seat on the cart, I let him go a bit further. But he mustn't get too tired. I usually rub methylated spirits into youngsters' legs where the hopples touch to harden the skin and prevent them chafing, and we smear udder cream all inside the hopples for the same reason. But I usually take the hopples off altogether and let him free-leg once he has learned to pace, though everybody has different methods. You really do have to know your horse. At this stage he ought to be driven every day with everything in place, but it will be months and months and months before he is asked for serious speed.'

Terry believes that breaking horses is mainly commonsense, and, though the youngsters are usually given hard feed as soon as they come in, it is not a high energy diet. 'Too much would make them too gassy to learn anything. But as they start to work harder, they get more.' Breaking is never without its mishaps, no matter how experienced you are or how much care you take. 'Gipsy ran away with me one of the first times I sat on the cart. The best ones usually have a bit of spirit! And even now, if you tie him up and take his bridle off before unhitching the cart, he'll climb the wall.'

Getting a youngster to pace is a headache for most people, but Terry finds that patience pays off. 'They are all different, and some will "roll over" and pace in two days, and some might take a week. I usually lunge them with the hopples on and get them to trot a bit faster, but they usually find their own beat, and once they do, I keep them to it and don't allow them to go any faster or slower. We shoe them with light plates in front and a bit of weight behind, right from the start and I think that helps. We might use a heavier shoe behind, or even just a pair of leather boots on the hind legs is sometimes enough to help them get their rhythm. As I said, I like to get them to free-leg pace without the hopples if possible. Apart from the chafing, it's sometimes hard to judge if a horse is lame with them on.'

Obviously, Terry has a wealth of experience in helping a youngster establish his pacing gait, and has the knack of knowing just how to encourage it. But for many it is weeks of trial and error, of pulling in the hopples a hole at a time (though a youngster should be encouraged to pace in as long a hopple as possible) or taking the overcheck up gradually, and certainly his action should be watched so that any help the farrier can give may be utilized. Sometimes the addition of a shadow-roll to the bridle can help, which stops a horse looking down and jumping shadows, but certainly a bucketful of patience is vital! Whatever happens, keep your cool and keep hold of his head. Trying to rush the horse along may only panic and unbalance him and you are trying to establish a co-ordinated rhythm. A recognized method of encouraging a youngster to pace is to drive on a slight downhill grade. But some pace better in a certain direction, or even uphill, and there are some who will 'roll over' and pace from day 1, so fingers crossed . . .

The training track at Russell's Cardiff yard is a small one, five circuits for a mile. When the youngsters begin their training on that track with Terry, they generally pace the mile in four minutes. Those that Russell and Terry consider good enough to go to the races and qualify keep pacing over the weeks until they cover the mile in three minutes. The youngster is still not asked for consistent speed, only in short bursts, perhaps over a quarter (of a mile), and the fastest he would be asked to pace over a mile before actually going to the races would be 2 minutes 25 seconds. This did not prevent Leckwith Pride recording 2 minutes 2 seconds as a two-year-old, and the Leckwith horses such as Gipsy (2.8.0) and Baron (2.6.0) achieving early success.

For a whole week prior to the race debut of the youngster, he has 'gate practice'. 'We've built a little starting gate which we fix on the back of Russell's Shogun, and we teach the youngsters to follow it with confidence. You always have to be prepared for them to spook at things, and they really need to know about the gate before they get to the races.'

A yearling which comes in to be broken in October at Russell's yard may be ready to run in a qualifying race as a two-year-old the following June if all goes according to plan. Those individuals who prove to be a little backward will be turned away to strengthen up and will probably be produced for the following season.

Breaking youngsters has very much to be played by ear. There are some types, notably those by Armbro Mystic, who need a holiday between being broken and being prepared for the circuits. Some horses need a physical and mental break from the rigours of education before coping with the demands of racing. The psychological effects of racing on a horse should never be neglected, particularly on a young horse, who is gaining first impressions that will probably colour how he feels about the job for the rest of his career. Terry points out that any problem such as boring (or hanging: leaning to one side or the other) should hopefully be eliminated as soon as it occurs. Indeed, it is very rare for a horse from Russell's yard to be seen wearing any corrective gadget such as a head-pole or burr.

Working a 'baby' in the middle of the track rather than just on the inner will help prevent this problem and stop him from anticipating the bends. A youngster should never finish his work sessions at the same point on the track, or he will begin to pull himself up there in the hope that his labours might end prematurely. It is always wise to carry a whip with a youngster, but it should only be used for encouragement and correction; giving vent to frustration with a whip is unforgivable. It won't make you feel any better, and the horse does not have the logic to understand anything other than immediate punishment for a misdemeanour. As some sage quoth, 'If whips could cure them, there wouldn't be any bad horses.'

Many people break a horse to ride before he is introduced to the cart, though this tends to be restricted to three-year-olds, unless a very light rider is available. If a horse is fully conversant with all the signals and commands

Things don't always go right, no matter how much care you take! Terry Laventure hits the deck at Huntley.

given by a 'jockey', he will respond to them, and, one hopes, feel more at ease with the cart when first introduced. Horses are generally broken to the saddle at some time during their competitive lives, as exercising can be done more easily when ridden, once they are past the stage of needing full regalia to operate. This also helps vary their routine and prevents them from becoming bored. (However, some Standardbreds seem to have a very high boredom threshold, and those that live in barns seeing little other than the horse opposite and the same old training track, whom you think would be brain-dead with apathy for the job, frequently go out and win week after week!) But riding a quiet, older horse upsides to 'nanny' a 'baby' on the track is often a good move because it gives him confidence and he will be less spooky.

Naturally, much depends on the type of horse you have as to how much racing he actually does as a two-year-old. There are some owners who would not race a horse until much later anyway. 'I don't think a two-year-old is mature enough to be racing at all,' commented Harry Taylor from Wreningham, 'it's sending a boy to do a man's job.'

John Howard, who has a string of good horses, including Howard's Way, also now believes in leaving them to grow. 'We ran Howard's Way at two in the Sires Stakes. He finished last. Now he's older, he's won us seventeen races.' Fosters Way was also only introduced to racing as a three-year-old and became a prolific winner for the Howard family.

'We don't usually run two-year-olds,' said Maureen Drysdale, mother of top Scottish drivers, George and William. 'In the past, when we have been tempted, we've always managed to pick the wrong one to train!'

So it is all down to good judgement and personal opinion. A quiet introduction to the excitement of the races cannot go amiss for a 'baby', and for those preparing foundations for the future, a few schooling runs for experience in qualifiers. But if you are the type of trainer who wants to win the first time your animal prints his mark on the track, good luck to you, because you will obviously have ensured you have the horsepower mature enough to achieve this. But it is a fact that the fast horses who bring home the bacon early in their careers rarely train on to be as brilliant later in life, but then maybe they wouldn't have if they had been left . . . who can say? Racing is a great leveller, and it is best to do what you personally believe in. But the true novice driver who wishes to get behind a two-year-old has a misplaced sense of adventure and would be better off with an experienced partner. It isn't as simple as driving a car, which many 'grandstand pilots' seem to imagine, and the gears on a youngster are decidedly shaky! Occasionally there is a brake failure, and the person on the end of the reins ideally ought to be well acquainted with such situations and know just how to manage the steering and throttle!

7

Trouble Shooting

Only the seriously deranged or the naively optimistic could possibly expect the way to the winners' circle to be completely unhindered by problems. The sad truth is, if you've got horses, you've got trouble of some sort! On the other hand, if you have purchased an older horse who has been trained from an early age on a raceway, the change of routine and scenery will probably do much to rejuvenate his resolve.

As with any equestrian activity, if a horse suddenly seems disinterested in giving the job his best shot, start looking for the physical cause before condeming him as 'doggy'. A blood test performed by your vet, which many trainers use as a regular indication of a horse's fitness, will pinpoint many things from viruses to muscle damage, and is well worth the investment. But keep an eye on the obvious things, his appetite, whether his urine is clear, whether he enjoys a roll. Especial attention should be paid to how he gets up after lying down; any stiffness or difficulty will pinpoint problems that may otherwise have escaped attention.

Should a horse begin consistently to 'break', particularly on bends, and cannot be improved by adjustment of the hopples and/or overcheck, or the anticipation of the driver, suspect shoulder or back pain if there is no obvious lameness. Harry Taylor, the 'Mr Trotting' of Norfolk and Suffolk, has a chiropracter to examine his horses once a month as a matter of course. He believes that too many trainers fail to detect their charges suffering problems in the spinal region. And just because a Standardbred is tougher than a Thoroughbred, there is no excuse for not running a hand down the legs every time you go in the box to try and detect early heat, just as you should for any performance horse.

Stevie Lees swears by knowing each horse as an individual, and if he suddenly changes his ordinary habits, even something as mundane as

If an usually well balanced horse begins to 'break' consistently, look for physical problems. Let us hope this is a one-off for Julie Bevan and It's a Joke at Broadheath.

staling in a different area of his box from usual, something may be amiss. As skilled trainer and driver, Ian Pimlott, points out, there is no great secret to training, it's just darned hard work, and such attention to detail is part and parcel of the quest for winners. But there are some problems that do have a solution in the form of an 'aid'. It cannot be stressed too strongly that all these 'gadgets' must be fitted absolutely correctly, or they will simply create a new set of difficulties. Sometimes it is a case of trial and error to see if anything can help, and it is wise to try out these things for the first time at home, and not suddenly discover at the races that a hood or whatever sends him half-batty. Admittedly, some horses do not necessarily need their head-pole, for instance, at home, but they do need to be used to it or it will only be another difficulty at the races.

Blinkers, also referred to as 'blinds' or 'shades', are an asset to any horse that spooks and shies in a race, or one that needs his concentration sharpening, or is panicked by the proximity of other runners. For the lazy types that only need them to keep their mind on their job, they are mostly best worked at home in an open bridle and the 'shades' only employed to sharpen them up. But be ready for a normally idle individual to become a lot keener at the races when he is 'closed down'. It is important that the blinkers on a 'blind' bridle are connected by a strap across the nose to prevent them being pulled out of position. They should not be too close to a horse's eyes, or the vision would be too restricted. Some people use the cloth, hood-type blinkers or visor as used by the Thoroughbred trainers. The advantage of these is that it is possible to adjust the cups around the eyes, and they are easier to use on a horse that only needs 'shades' actually at the races, instead of having to fiddle with attaching and unattaching them from the bridle.

A telescope bridle has round blinds resembling glasses which fit right round the eye, which must be exactly in the centre. This is used on horses who shy at wheels, or are unsettled by something in the region of their legs,

Trewly Surprising with a shadow-roll extending to his Kant-See-Baks to limit his downward vision, but not restrict vision forward or sideways.

sometimes the result of having been brought down in a race. Kant-See-Baks, which are often used on youngsters, are a form of blinker that does not obscure side vision, but merely prevents horses from looking back to see what the driver is doing, or being upset by their own cart. The same effect can be achieved by a sheepskin roll wrapped around the cheekpieces of the bridle directly behind the eyes.

A shadow roll or 'bluff' is a must for horses who are prone to jumping shadows or figments of their imaginations, because this is a very hairy pastime whilst wearing hopples. The shadow-roll is a thick sheepskin nose-band which prevents a horse from seeing the ground, and there are different widths and lengths to suit the individual, depending on just how spooky he is. Since it is more than advantageous for a horse to be able to see where it is going, the shadow-roll should only be adjusted when a horse has his head checked-up. Some of them are thinner in the middle to allow a clear forward vision. If adjusting the overcheck, don't forget to alter the shadow-roll, otherwise another problem could be created by the horse turning his head in an effort to see something other than the clouds. For an outrageous 'boggler', a brush roll is worth a try. It has bristles of about four inches or so glued to the noseband which constantly move in the breeze and either distract the horse or accustom it to ghosties. But if a horse continually has problems seeing 'pink elephants', particularly if he has previously been a Christian soul, get the vet to check his eyesight, as cataracts can sometimes cause a horse to see shadows.

Naturally, much depends on the temperament of the beast, but some horses get very wound up in the early stages of a race and become difficult to control. The noise of the other runners close to him can often wind him up, and stuffing his ears with cotton wool or using a hood or ear-muffs can alleviate this problem. Some horses object strongly to having their ears stuffed, and prefer a hood. But if employing cotton wool, make sure it is all removed afterwards, and that no fragments are left to cause infections and suchlike. Poppers are 'bobbles' attached to a cord which stuff the horse's ears to keep him calm during the initial stages of a race, but are pulled out by a thread when the driver sees fit to galvanize him to optimum effort and the noise and excitement around him can be utilized to help with the adrenalin surge.

There are many horses, particularly those who are rushed as 'babies', who hang one way or another on the track. Once you are certain there is no medical reason for it, there are various remedies depending on the severity of the problem. The head-pole is the most common deterrent. This is a small pole, roughly the size of a pool cue, with a telescoping extension, which is used to keep the horse's head straight. If a horse cocks his head to the right,

Debbie Birbeck is delighted with her Appleby win with Saunders Vandella, who wears a head-pole.

which is not uncommon, the pole must be fastened to the opposite side, the left, and vice versa. A piece of leather must be fastened to the saddle pad, anchored to the turret, which runs through a slit in the end of the pole and fastens to the overcheck hook on the top of the saddle pad. The other end of the pole clips onto a ring in front of the cheekpiece on an inner bridle, which is just like a cavesson noseband that has rings in strategic positions and is worn separately under the normal bridle. To be fitted correctly, the pole must be fastened outside the cheekpiece, and the inner bridle must be at least three fingers' width above the driving bit so that it does not impede its action. Sometimes a metal piece (referred to as a 'shoulder') is fitted to the

Ian Pimlott and Precious Fella, trained by Charlie McKenzie, winning the Famous Musselburgh Pace. Precious Fella wears a rein or line burr to help keep his head straight.

saddle pad to keep the pole higher and more rigid. Occasionally a horse may not respect the head-pole and will lean on it so that it does not have full effect; then a burr, a six-inch prickly strip, should be wrapped around it where it comes in contact with the neck. A rein (or line) burr works on the same principle but is laced around a normal stiffened rein and some horses prefer it to a head-pole.

There is a multitude of bits to counteract the difficulty of hanging, as with every other problem in the equestrian world! Maybe some of them even work, particularly the slip-mouth sidelining type, which are telescopic and provide extra leverage. It goes without saying that the teeth should always be eliminated as the cause of any problem. There have also been cases of horses who receive shocks from the effect of a metal bit creating static electricity on the teeth – imagine the reaction to that! And when all else has failed and horsemen have been tearing their hair out with frustration at being unable to detect the cause of the trouble, the simple change to either a rubber or nathe bit has wrought a minor miracle.

There are also plenty of bits designed to help contain a 'puller' in a race; advice is best sought on this problem from a reliable trainer. For a fierce puller, a lip cord is a possibility, unless the driver has hands like blacksmith's feet, but it is a device not widely used in the UK. This is a round cord which runs over the gums under the upper lip. The two ends of the cord then pass behind the driving bit on each side before buckling beneath the chin. When it is adjusted properly, pressure on the bit via the reins automatically causes the cord to press on the gums, acting on a nerve in the region which (supposedly!) quietens the horse. But a driver needs the hands of an angel for this to be fully effective. And if not adjusted properly, it is likely to send the animal frantic!

A lip cord must not be confused with a tongue-tie. This is used to stop a horse lolling his tongue around in his mouth and attempting to get it over the bit, which would result in a serious lack of control. Most of these unsavoury habits with the tongue, as with horses from all disciplines, are down to anxiety and excitement at the event where they know they are required to perform. And it is easy to be caught out by a horse getting his tongue over the bit at the start of a race who has shown no inclination to do so at home. Some wind problems due to soft-palate or laryngeal paralysis are occasionally helped by the application of a tongue-tie or strap, if an operation is undesirable. A straightforward soft leather tongue-strap can be purchased from any saddler and is widely used by Thoroughbred trainers. To apply it, the tongue is grasped and passed through a loop in the strap, which is then pulled tight enough to hold the tongue in position, but without being tight enough to be uncomfortable, or, God forbid, cut off the circulation. The tongue should never discolour, and, if unsure, get advice, preferably from a vet. There is currently no veterinary inspection of tongue-straps on harness racehorses, as there is with Thoroughbreds, though it is obvious that any horse who is unhappy with a contraption in his mouth will not be attaining its full potential. Some people use a soft crepe bandage as a tongue-tie, but the strap is less hassle, providing it is kept soft, because it is easier to get the tension just right once it has been fitted initially.

Some horses who are not prone to bearing down with their heads, do not require a check (or roof) bit, and their head is kept up by a chin strap which is buckled to the overcheck, but there are more horses who need a check bit than don't. For those who insist on leaning onto the check, there are a variety of different check bits to prevent it, though it is rare to see the more complicated sorts in the UK.

One of the answers to a horse that throws its head in the air to evade control is a martingale, as it would be for any other performance horse. The basic standing martingale, running directly from the girth to the bottom ring on the inner bridle is possibly the most widely employed on the UK circuits. An elastic insert to allow a certain amount of play is fairly fashionable, and the bottom strap is usually sheepskin-covered to prevent chafing between the forelegs. Occasionally, a horse can sometimes touch its knee

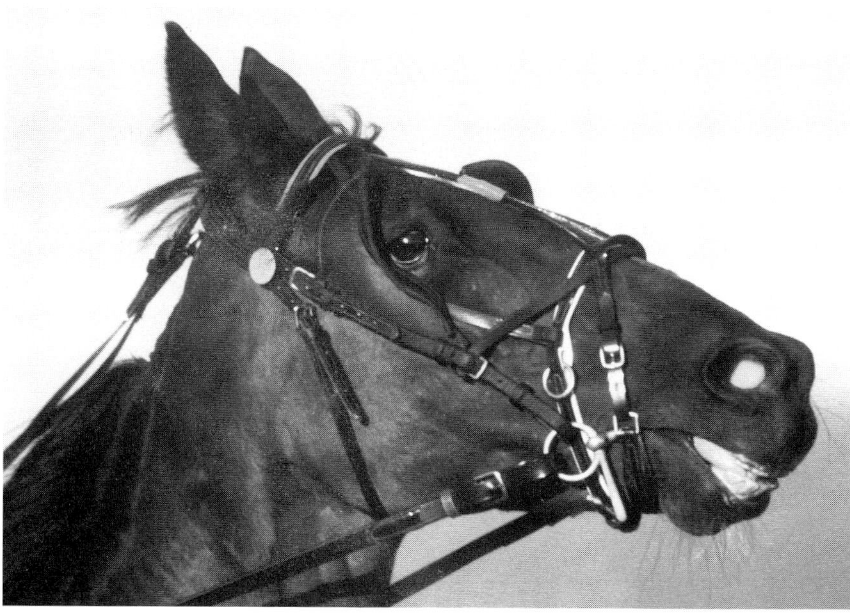

Turbo does not require a check (or roof) bit but has a chin-strap to keep his head up.

with an opposite hind foot (cross-firing) in the rough and tumble of a race, but unfortunately there are also horses which are confirmed knee-knockers, their front foot catching the opposite knee, usually at speed. Naturally, it isn't only the sheer physical damage that is caused that is the problem here, but a horse with this kind of action who consistently hurts himself will soon decide to call it a day in his races. Remedial shoeing can help with both these problems, but persistent knee-knockers are a pain and should be extensively booted with decent protection. Some knee boots can have suspenders attached, which clip onto front and back of each boot and pass over the withers, so that they do not have to be buckled around the leg quite so tightly. Another attempt to keep the forelegs apart in stride are 'spreaders', some tube-like straps which encircle each foreleg and fasten to the shafts of the cart. Unfortunately, they tend to chafe a sensitive-skinned horse very easily.

These are some of the problems more specific to the pacer; needless to say, they also suffer the setbacks common to any normal horse! All these aids have their place, and some horses would not run successfully without their help, but before resorting to such things, make doubly sure that there is no physical cause of the problem. If this were the case, or if the head-pole or whatever were incorrectly fitted, you would have twice as much trouble.

8

The Major Tracks

In the first decade of the 20th century, 'trotting' was popular enough to warrant having several thriving hard tracks. These were mainly in highly populated areas: Greenford Driving Park, the hub of the well supported London Trotting Club, held weekly meetings at Ealing, and Manchester boasted two tracks, Moorside (Droylsden) and Audenshaw. Mrs Leonard Jones was the first lady to ever drive in a harness race at Greenford Park, in 1930. On October 9th in the same year, the first ladies driving race was staged there and attracted the attention of the national media, and a cinematograph film was even made of it. Six ladies started for the Silver Trophy Race. Miss Byron drove 'a splendid race' with the favourite, Mr Gavin Shanks's Volo Jay, to make all and win from May Duffy, driven by sixteen-year-old Miss Vera Salter. It was a popular win. Miss Byron, a Surrey horsewoman who had been associated with flat racehorses, was a well known figure at Greenford, where she also raced the greyhounds that she owned and trained.

To complement these meetings, there were also numerous grass meetings all over the UK, usually held in conjunction with agricultural shows or sports.

The hard tracks usually held different events on their circuits on other nights; at Greenford it was greyhound racing, and at Moorside it was a motorcycle speedway. Unfortunately, though they were all busy, profitable tracks, almost all suffered the same fate – the lease expired and the landowner sold the site for development. Down the years it has been the same, sad story. Kendal Raceway, which graduated from being a popular grass venue to a highly efficient hard track, was another casualty in the early 1990s; a supermarket now stands where fast horses and their drivers battled for supremacy at the wire. The best class of racing was staged there, the cards were always full and spectators were happy. Owing to the efforts of

One of harness racing's great trainers, Edmund Dodd, on his trotting pony, Erl, having won at Blackpool.

Joan Prickett and Geoff Sedgewick, amongst others, Kendal did much to cement the sport. But nothing, it seems, can gainsay the inexorable 'march of progress' and the history of harness racing is littered with memories of tracks that are no more. Their closure, in turn, demoralized owners who would have to travel many miles to enjoy their racing, which would make their continuing involvement an uneconomical proposition.

In the 1990s, with the advent of Dunstall Park promising better prize money and extensive media coverage, and many Thoroughbred people turning their attentions to harness racing, the sport is set to rise like a phoenix from the ashes. Let us hope that the promoters have learned the harsh lesson of putting all their eggs in one basket; there is room in the sport for everyone. The trick is learning to all pull in the same direction at the same time.

Arguably (particularly to grass-track enthusiasts), hard-track racing is the professional side of the sport. The firmer surfaces ensure faster racing, and the best times. It is only on the raceways (hard tracks) that the two-minute barrier is in jeopardy, and where the national records are broken. Often the top-class horses have a long, low action that is not so well suited to grass and they can only achieve ultimate performance on the hard circuits. Obviously, promoters of the raceways have invested a great deal of money in their facilities, and the major tracks have stabling from which horses are trained. Though harness racing supporters are usually affable creatures by nature, they tend to have an allegiance to either hard or grass tracks, even though it is obvious that both have their place.

Some hard-track promoters, who provide racing from April until January, are occasionally less than complimentary about grass meetings who only have to fund one or two fixtures a year on their venue. *Plus sa change*! An extract from the *Trotting World And Horse Review* on May 25th, 1929, reads:

> It is surprising and disappointing for the promoters of regular all the year round light-harness horse meetings, to see a grass-track meeting such as Appleby, Westmorland, receive an entry of 54 trotting horses from all over the country for their annual meeting on Whit Monday. At the Audenshaw (Manchester) meeting on the same day, only 16 horses were entered (12 starting) for a handicap as valuable as that given at Appleby. This hardly seems fair, as the regular tracks keep the sport together throughout the year, holding many meetings on unsatisfactory

Miss Prim, driven by George Dodd and owned by Mr Whittaker, who won the £1,000 trotting handicap on 9th, 10th and 11th October, 1922, at Audenshaw Stadium, Manchester.

> dates at a financial loss, in order to assist those connected with the sport, only for the outside occasional meetings to avail themselves of the best holiday fixtures, and reap the benefits of others hard work and patience. Without the regular tracks keeping the sport together through dull times, these meetings could not be held.

And this was written long before all our current hard-track promoters were even born. Grass meetings frequently provide the 'nursery' for both the horses and drivers who grace the hard circuits, and are also more of a family day out for the spectators. It is certainly 'horses for courses', and, though the zealous declare that the future of the sport lies solely at Dunstall Park, Tir Prince and the other raceways, there are plenty who will remain loyal to grass fixtures and who are just as keen to see things move forward.

Tir Prince Raceway

Tir Prince Raceway at Towyn, near Rhyl in North Wales, is a superb hard circuit where racing follows the American style, and the floodlit track is a copy of Freestate Raceway, USA, which is one of the fastest in the world. Half a mile in circumference, with an all-weather surface of washed sand and limestone dust, the track is wide enough to take eight horses off the gate in comfort and safety. The bends are long, and the whole track is banked to encourage speed, yet minimize accidents.

The set-up is the brainchild of businessman and farmer, Billy Williams, who tirelessly promotes the two weekly meetings which are held in the summer months, reducing to one a week in the winter when the wind blows unforgivingly off the sea. The sea was almost the death of the whole project in February 1990, when the terrible floods that breached the sea wall and engulfed the town washed away the newly constructed circuit which had been built on fifty acres of previously derelict land that Billy had leased from Colwyn Borough Council. For many, this shocking natural disaster would have been the end of all the hopes and dreams, but Billy (as many have discovered to their cost) is made of sterner stuff. The grandstand would have to wait, but the track would be rebuilt. And so it was, at a further cost of £50,000, and the raceway was opened only three weeks behind schedule, on May 22nd, 1990. Billy feels that the venue on the North Wales coast is a particularly poignant one, since Prestatyn, where the roots of affiliated harness racing began, is only a few miles away.

It was at Prestatyn that Billy first got hooked on harness racing. He was invited to a meeting there in the early 1960s and was completely mesmerized by the sport. Before he left the raceway, he had swapped his Cortina car

Track promoter of Tir Prince Raceway, Billy Williams, with race secretary, Wendy Fairclough, and Oliver, who leads out the runners.

for a harness racehorse called Sorrento and all his gear. 'I raced him myself twenty-five times that first year, and we finished second on twenty-two of those runs. It was then that I realized that I needed glasses . . .

That was the beginning of a lifelong passion for Billy. He has trained and driven ever since. In 1987, he bred, trained and drove the British Trotting Champion, Buck's Fizz, and in 1990 drove Ynys Lyn to victory in the Prakas Derby. And he is not the only driver in the family. His glamorous wife, Norma, has a couple of ladies races to her credit and his son, Billy Jnr., is fast becoming one of the raceway's best drivers. Billy senior is now a BHRC steward. There are some fifty boxes in barn accommodation adjacent to the track, and trainers from all over the country base themselves there for the season. James Murdock and Jane Paterson are among the most successful handlers who train on the Towyn track, and Stevie Lees is consistently leading driver at the circuit. Sian Gresley-Jones frequently flies the flag for the ladies in the Tir Prince winners' circle, and is usually top of the females table. Mary Wadham's Saunders Glitter was the most prolifically winning horse at the circuit in 1993, and Tony Cotton's stallion, Jeff's Comfort, was the best trotter. Ted's Way, trained by ex-boxer, Bernie Lloyd, was voted the best track horse. The impressive total of £129,705 in prize money was paid out during that season by the raceway.

Since its opening, many of the Classic races had been staged there, including the National Pacing Derby, but the tender for prize money offered for these important races was exceeded in 1994 by Dunstall Park, who will now stage all Classic races except for the Roosevelt Cup.

In 1993, live television and radio coverage commenced for the Tuesday evening meetings, and revolutionized the sport in Wales and beyond, making many of the professional drivers household names.

Wendy Fairclough took on the job as secretary a few weeks after the raceway opened and has been there ever since, organizing the mountain of paperwork connected with the flourishing fixtures. The dry-humoured commentator, Peter Lees, enhances the atmosphere of pulsing excitement with his charismatic and well informed narrations.

Tir Prince Raceway is situated near the sea-front at Towyn, on south side of A548, two miles east of its junction with A55, two miles east of Rhyl.

Corbiewood

Corbiewood Stadium, near Bannockburn in Scotland, was built by the Taylor Brothers in the late 1960s. It is currently owned by metal merchant, David Morton Senior, an ardent supporter of the sport. A successful trainer himself, David has been responsible for many major winners, including Stepaway, the hero of the 1993 Appleby Spring Meeting. His daughter-in-law, Helen, was in fact the first lady to drive the winner of the Famous Musselburgh Pace in 1991 with Red Governess. This was a poignant moment indeed for David, whose horses had been second in the Final on no less than seven occasions. In recent years David has extended the floodlit Corbiewood track and updated the facilities, and it is now one of the most consistently popular venues for hard-track racing in the country. The crowd is both enthusiastic and knowledgeable, and the bookmakers are willing to take substantial wagers, which is not always the case elsewhere. Much of this happy state of affairs is due to the energetic and diplomatic management of the track promoter, Ian Armstrong.

Ian, owner of the printing company which supplies the colourful race-cards, reveals his age as 'fifty, plus VAT!' He also has his sport at heart rather than just in his pocket, and is a successful owner and breeder. He made a gift

Ann Lynch, owner of prolific winner, Ambro Fling, with Ian Armstrong, promoter of Corbiewood Stadium, who gave her the horse and the Drysdale brothers, George (left) *and Willie* (right) *in the winners' enclosure at Carlisle.*

of Armbro Fling to his girlfriend, Ann Lynch, and she has had the pleasure of watching the horse become a top class Free-for-All contender who has broken the track record twice at Errol with Willie Drysdale. Because Corbiewood is a shorter track, approximately 660 yards, the tactics of driving a race there are absolutely crucial. The banked bends come quickly, so it is important to be in a good position early in the race, and top driver, Mike Lord, relates that it is unusual for a horse to come and win from too far off the pace (too far behind the leaders).

Because of its tight bends and short straights, it is rare to record very fast times at Corbiewood, though the track record is an amazing 2 minutes, 2.6 seconds set by McGuigan and George Drysdale. Though maybe not as popular with the drivers, this very construction is what adds to the excitement of the spectators, for the runners are never far away.

The judge, Mr Jack Magiure, has been part of the harness racing scene for a great many years, and another colourful character of the sport, Alistair Smith, handles the secretarial side of things at the stadium with skill and efficiency; Davie Douglas, the commentator, sounds as if he would be equally at home at his job on the North American circuits.

There are half a dozen or so trainers who operate from the track, the leading exponent being Jim McInally. Helped by the inexhaustable Mandy Stanley, Jim enjoyed his most successful season ever in 1993. Jim also took

On the gate at York Raceway.

the leading driver award at Corbiewood, and other consistently successful pilots include Robert Wilson, Mike Lord, Willie Greenhorn Jnr., the Drysdale brothers, George and Willie, Russell Collinson, Jock Ritchie, George Kerr, Gregor and Hugh Menzies, Alec McDonald and Clare Bousefield.

The stadium stages two- and three-year old championships annually, and regularly attracts runners from Ireland, England and Wales, as well as the full quota of locals. Meetings are run every Thursday evening from April until the New Year, and also on the Monday and Friday of Musselburgh week in August.

It is situated on west side of A91, mid-way between M9 and A9, a mile south of Bannockburn. And is well worth the trip to enjoy the ready hospitality of the natives!

York Raceway

One of the fastest raceways in the country, York has a history of important records having been broken at its meetings. Golden Dale and Alan Haythornthwaite have twice set a UK mile record here in under two minutes. The track is half a mile in circumference and forty-five feet in width, and is a popular venue with many trainers, particularly John Gill, Granville Ainley and Joe Sowerby.

York Raceway was built in 1978 under the direction of Arthur Slack, Jimmy Birch, Ronnie Harrop, Colin Johnson and Sid Harker, but in 1985 three of the partners pulled out and the stadium was sold to Lord Keegan, the current owner. Lord Keegan promoted racing for a season before handing the reins to Barry Delaney, a seasoned owner and breeder of Standardbred horses in 1992.

Early in 1994 York Harness Racing Club was formed of thirty-plus supporters who offered financial support to the raceway and took over the lease. A management committee of a dozen stalwarts was set up to deal with the administration of the racing. This was chaired by Barry Gray, owner of the superb performer, Afton Dream, who was BHRC Horse Of The Year in 1992, having won a brilliant succession of races that included the National Pacing Derby. Sheila Jackson was the inaugural treasurer, and Barry Delaney remained on the management committee. With owners, trainers and drivers working together for the good of their sport, YHRC is framing races that will appeal to everyone, including events on the card restricted to mares only. The careful structuring of races will result in better racing, and improve the chances for owners to win prize money.

York is a favourite track of class driver, Mike Lord, who is part of the management committee, as is another driver with a good strike rate there, Trevor Brown. Others often in the winners' enclosure include Stuart Sowerby, John Hunt, Watson Harrop, Bill Armer and Alan Haythornthwaite. Harness racing generally opens the season at York on the first Saturday in April and meetings continue most (but not all) Saturdays throughout the summer, with the occasional Bank Holiday fixture thrown in.

The raceway is situated 9 miles west of York in Pool Lane, which runs north off the A59 a mile before Green Hammerton.

Dunstall Park, Wolverhampton

On April 9th, 1994, the $^{5}/_{8}$ths harness racing circuit was officially opened at Dunstall Park, Wolverhampton racecourse. The £16.7 million development was masterminded by R.A.M. Racecourses, the firm of Richard and Ron Muddle, who made such a success of all-weather Thoroughbred racing at Southwell.

The crushed limestone circuit is situated inside the Thoroughbred tracks, and harness racing alternates with flat racing every Saturday throughout the year, and is staged under floodlights on Thursday evenings from the end of May. The lighting system, which was unveiled at a Thoroughbred fixture on Boxing Day, 1993, was installed by the main suppliers to the North American racing industry. It includes no less than 32 miles of electrical cable, 90,000 lb of steel poles and half a million lb of concrete. The full mode is 1,200 lux, the equivalent of 50,000 car headlights. The photo

Horses lining up for the start of the first-ever harness race at Dunstall Park on April 9th, 1994.

finish has a special facility of 64,000 watts of incandescent light. Most of the Classic races are currently staged at Dunstall Park, including the National Pacing Derby, The Prakas Series, The Sires Stakes and the National Pacing Futurity. The safety factor is uppermost in the minds of both Richard Muddle and his harness racing manager, Mick Wilcox, and, though the track is wide enough to accommodate more, they only allow eight horses on the gate. The bends have a 10 per cent banking, and the exciting free-for-all principle of racing is utilized whenever possible.

There are facilities for 130 horses to be stabled at Dunstall Park, with on-site accommodation for twenty professional trainers.

The circuit is in easy reach of the main arterial road network of the UK, being close to the M54, M6, M5 and A5, and directly linked with the A449. It is situated at Dunstall Park, Gorsebrook Road, Dunstall, Wolverhampton.

Amman Valley Trotting Club

The circuit at Gwaun-Cae-Gurwen, near Ammanford, is of similar dimensions (656 yards) to Corbiewood, but is not floodlit. Eight fixtures a year are staged here, with its major meeting on August Bank Holiday Monday. It is managed by a very active and supportive club committee which was formed

Action at Amman Valley; Raymond Jenkins and First Edition lead the field.

in 1980, though the track was raced on long before that, as the minutes show that 'Ammanford' applied for affiliation to the newly formed National Harness Racing Club in 1969. Joe Perry was the inaugural chairman of the AVTC but Eric Jones was elected soon after and remained at the helm until his retirement in 1994. His wife, Betty, who had been the inexhaustible secretary since 1982, bowed out at the same time, and this husband and wife team was replaced by another, Mr and Mrs Alf Launchbury. The track record is held by Russell Andrew's Leckwith Gipsy, who recorded 2 minutes 8 seconds in an intermediate race in 1993, piloted by Terry Laventure, who was also leading driver there in the same year.

Huw Thomas has won a lot of races here as a trainer and driver over many years, and others with good strike rates on the track are Tony Richards, Roy Wilson, Paul Evans, Alf Launchbury, Steve Flook and Jeff Langford.

The circuit is situated at Tairgwaith. From A474 at Gwaun-Cae-Gurwen, take A4069 and turn right immediately.

Appleby

The Appleby Spring Meeting at the end of May is hugely popular with both drivers and spectators alike; its ancestry goes back to a Sports Day. Held under the auspices of the Eden Valley Trotting Association, the meeting has always been associated with the Bousefield family. The half-mile grass track is on Holme Field, Appleby-In-Westmorland, the home of Chris (Kit) Bousefield, and his brother, Jack Bousefield, who rode his first winner at the age of ten in 1927, is President of the meeting. 'I got out of school at three o'clock, rode my pony twelve miles to the meeting, won the heat, got beat in the final, and then rode twelve miles home . . .' he recalled.

The region is well populated with staunch supporters of harness racing, and in the early 1920s, there were two or three fixtures held every summer in the area. When Appleby British Legion planned to hold an athletics meeting at the Bousefields' farm, it was suggested that a 'trotting' and pony racing event was held in conjunction, and in 1923, a small committee was formed to organize it. It was held on Whit Monday, and became widely known as the 'Whit Monday Trot', the culmination of a week of fixtures, of which only Hawes and Appleby remain. In 1929, it is recorded in the *Trotting World And Horse Review* that seven thousand spectators attended Appleby Races and Sports, to watch an entry of fifty-four trotting horses, which also included pacers. The £105 Open Handicap was won by a length by 'the black pacing mare, Miss Woolworth, owned by Mr J. Dunlop, who had been defeated in its heat by the trotter Jack Fox'. Jack Fox was a British-

Jim McInally, leading trainer and driver in Scotland, winning at Appleby's Brough meeting with Bob Kennedy's Surprise Skipper.

Young Morecombe winning Appleby spring races with Clem Dodd in the 1960s, floating over the ground (note, no foot is in contact).

bred trotter who regularly won first-class handicaps.

After the War, there were fewer 'trotters' around, and most racing was 'galloping' in the region, though Scotland still had plenty of harness racehorses. The legendary horse Hurricane was persuaded to come and give an exhibition to rekindle the interest in the sport, and the Appleby committee were pressed to give as much prize-money as they could possibly afford to improve the situation. Today, the meeting still attracts the very best horses and drivers. When Noel Simpson built the hard track at Prestatyn and the Night Trotting Club was formed in the early 1960s, closely followed by the United Kingdom Trotting Association and The National Harness Racing Club, Appleby dropped the galloping races from its fixtures and became affiliated to the fore-runner of the BHRC.

'There was a lot of fun in the job in those days, even if times were hard,' mused Jack Bousefield, who, now in his mid-seventies, has only recently given up driving, though he and Kit still own horses that are trained by son, John, and driven by niece, Clare, and granddaughter, Diane, with great success.

Appleby track has recently been extended to prevent the bend coming too quickly after the start, and because most of the races are handicaps at Appleby, Jack does not set much store by a track record. 'The fastest horses are trailing too far,' he explained, 'and with the course recently being altered, I honestly don't know what the track record is.' With the Bousefields standing two of the first stallions imported from the USA, High Point and Hodgens Surprise, to improve the Standardbred breed in this country, they have done much to further harness racing over the years. One of their favourite mares, April Star, won 52 races in her career, one of them owing (handicapped) 32 seconds in a saddle race, and her great-grandson, Ginger Tom, is a class horse today.

Appleby Spring Meeting is where everyone in harness racing would like to win, and the huge crowds that attend are a fitting tribute to the foresight of that small committee in 1923 who wished to stage a success. There are several established trainers in the Appleby area apart from the Bousefields, including Arthur and Evelyn Slack and Jim Winter.

There are two other meetings held there, in June and August, and the access road to the track can be found off the B6542, near its junction with the A66.

Musselburgh

Another highlight of the harness racing calendar, Musselburgh is one of the toughest fixtures, and the only track in the country where races are run on the right-hand rein. The eleven furlongs, run on Edinburgh racecourse, are a searching test of a horse's stamina, and, though the two-day meeting is held the second week in August, it is often wet enough to make the going sticky, so that runners really do have to 'get the trip'.

It is also one of the most vividly colourful fixtures, being a true 'fair day' with entertainments and amusements that remind Thoroughbred supporters of Epsom on Derby Day.

The Musselburgh Fair Day Races evolved in 1893 from an ancient custom practised on Musselburgh Links to protect the burgh's rights and privileges, known as the 'riding of the marches'. Such was the enthusiasm at the races that some of the leading citizens of the day formed a Musselburgh Fair Day Association, and Mr Andrew McIntosh was appointed to head a deputation to the Town Council. Permission was readily given for use of the racecourse and to allow the pitching of marquees on the links and in the paddock, though the request for a donation towards the expenses of the event was just as rapidly refused!

The aims of the association were recorded as, 'To provide within the burgh of Musselburgh, races for horses etc.. . . To encourage, by the giving of prizes or otherwise, merchants or others within the burgh of Musselburgh to keep smart horses, ponies, vehicles and others . . .

'To engender and foster the feeling of kindness to animals, and to

A heat at Musselburgh in the 1960s. The winner was driven by Jimmy Young, Clem Dodd drove the second horse (Young Morecombe) and Bobby Craig rode the third horse.

encourage the proper grooming of horses and the cleaning and keeping of horses . . .

'To provide within the Burgh of Musselburgh, amusements, recreations and games of skill and facilities for the same and to maintain and improve the amenity of Musselburgh and the parish of Inveresk.'

The Association's first Fair Day meeting was held on the Fair Day in August, 1894, and was an outstanding success that has continued ever since.

At these early fixtures, the races were mainly local events, races for merchant's ponies, a cycle race, a match between the carthorses of Hickman and Downie, and a donkey race where owners rode their opponents' donkeys and the last donkey past the post was the winner. This was superbly entertaining, with jockeys employing all kinds of wiles to galvanize their mounts, including carrots and the beating of drums, and one jockey even played the melodion from the saddle! Because the course was open in those days, it was ideal for families to picnic, making it a gay occasion for all who attended.

Gradually, the local events were phased out and replaced by open trotting and galloping races which attracted runners from all over the UK and abroad, which in turn generated even more spectators to enjoy the unique atmosphere. The association has always played a very active part in the community, making dozens of donations to various worthy causes, and it is recorded that it 'subscribed nobly to war efforts such as the Spitfire Fund and The Aid To Russia Fund . . .' among other things.

Naturally, the directors have a responsibility to maintain traditions, but of late the reputation of organizing a meeting that is the mecca of harness racing in the United Kingdom has become of prime importance.

The famous Musselburgh Pace and the Hope Trophy are two of the most coveted prizes in the harness racing calendar, the final being worth £5,000 to the winner.

The First World War caused the postponement of the meeting in 1914–18, but the only other fixture loss was in 1897, due to a waterlogged course.

In 1985, there was a dead heat for the Famous Musselburgh Pace when the horses The Lucky One and Bye For Now crossed the line together, but the atmosphere of the meeting is such that *all* finishes invoke unbridled enthusiasm from the substantial crowd.

Clem Dodd, now in his late seventies, was one of the most talented drivers that the sport has ever seen, and won no less than thirteen major races at Musselburgh in his career. These were victories in either the Famous Musselburgh Pace, the Trots, or Invitation Races. His pacing winners included Lucy in the 1930s, Silver Star in 1950, Young Morecombe, Newport Hanover and Cole's Star in the 1960s and Turn Of The Tide and Saunders Admiral in the 1970s. The trotters that took Musselburgh honours with Clem were Young Steven, Fluck's Garbo and Yankee Doodle (twice).

Phyllis James, the daughter of well respected trainer, Bill Evans, also had an excellent record of riding winners at Musselburgh, scoring on Bento Hollandia on four occasions in the late 1960s and early 1970s. This was made all the more impressive as there were then few women in the sport. Phyllis has only recently retired from race-driving, having driven winners in at least six different countries whilst representing the UK, including breaking a track record in Finland. And Bento Hollandia, happy and healthy in his middle age, is still with Phyllis and her husband Derek at their home in South Wales.

The winner of the prestigious Centenary Famous Musselburgh Pace in 1993 was an especially memorable one. Helen Sinclair's five-year-old, Johnnies Decision, had been laid up with an injury since his victory in the National Pacing Derby in 1991, apart from an unimpressive run at Appleby earlier in 1993. The Drysdale family from Forest Mill in Scotland were on tenterhooks while training the brilliant horse, well aware of the truth in the saying that, 'Nothing happens to the bad 'uns.' Ian, George and Willie did their job perfectly in producing the horse on top of his form on the day, and he cruised home from some very fancied horses to take his heat with George on the sulky seat. 'To win the heat was what we had hoped,' smiled Ian, 'The Final was a real bonus!'

Musselburgh is the place where legends are made and fairy tales can come true, if you are but brave enough to dream! It is certainly the meeting place for every harness racing supporter from throughout the UK for that Tuesday and Wednesday in August, and a venue where all the factors are so uncertain that the bookmakers are never afraid to take substantial bets. Carole Auld, herself a seasoned competitor, has been race secretary since the mid-1980s, though David Holmes has recently taken on her duties as secretary to the Association, of which Mr W. McAlpine has been President for many years.

The track can be found on the north side of the A199, five miles east of central Edinburgh.

Wreningham

This half-mile Norfolk track is the only grass circuit in the UK that is raced on as regularly as a hard track. Harry Taylor has been the driving force behind the promotion and continuation of the sport in East Anglia and beyond. He explained how Wreningham came into being: 'There were very few meetings in East Anglia when I was young, except for a bit of road racing amongst the dealing type of people, which I had nothing to do with. But there were a few trotting ponies about, mainly Icelandic ponies, and there was a local doctor, Dr Darrell, from All Saints Green in Norwich who was famous for the trotting pony he used to have in a gig to do his rounds. He even used it in a sleigh when it snowed, there were several pictures of him in the pubs roundabout.

'But of course, there were flourishing tracks in London at Greenford and Wembley, and in Manchester, and in the 1950s, after my father had died and I had got married, and served my time in the forces, I wanted to get involved with trotters again. I started by organizing little meetings at shows such as Diss, and on airfields. It wasn't top-class racing, but we had our fun out of the sport. Then Fred Fairclough, Tom Mitchell, Arthur Lannon, who had the very good horse, Cheerio, and I formed the East Anglia Trotting Company Ltd.

'We rented the Firs Speedway Stadium just outside Norwich, which had all the facilities and was a lovely banked track with a good surface. It cost £60 a night to rent in those days, in 1958, and we charged spectators six shillings to get in. We were a bit short of horses, but still had a good card, with eighteen horses running twice a night, three races over a mile, and then three over a mile and a quarter. The prize money we gave was £25 to the winner, £15 for second and £5 for third, and it cost £3 to enter for the two races. So it was actually good prize money in comparison to nowdays, since a gallon of diesel only cost 1/3d (just over 5p) a gallon then, and you could get your horse shod for a pound. And the expense of keeping him was much less too! We were well supported by such people as Bill Hunt from Doncaster, and Fred Fairclough had a really good horse called Morgan Spencer, who won everywhere. Because we had aroused so much interest at The Firs, there was quite a good circuit of fixtures organized in East Anglia between 1958 to 1965. There was Foxwell Stadium in Ipswich, and meetings at Kings Lynn, Yarmouth, Skegness and Boston, and Dick Saunders, who owned the Grand National winner, Grittar, also held a meeting. But then Prestatyn opened and things got harder. We raced at The Firs every Thursday night, and we did make money, but then the new ruling body of the sport, the National Harness Racing Club, decreed that racing could not be staged on hard tracks that were under half a mile in circumference, and our exciting racing had to stop.

'We kept going with low prize money at little meetings promoted by Johnny West of Gravesend, and Mr Jenkins who held a few in Kent and Sussex, and I was holding regular meetings on my own track at Taysborough. It wasn't classy but we all enjoyed the racing.

'Then I was approached by a local horse show committee to put on a demonstration, and I had to explain about the stipulation of the tracks having to be large enough. I must have been quite a salesman of the sport, because that committee, which included Elisabeth Blazak, who is now a stipendary steward of the BHRC, got very keen, and formed an association. Twelve people put £300 each in and obtained the ex-motor racing circuit at Snetterton as their racing venue, there being just enough grass to set up a track. We held a very successful meeting there in 1980, the very first one that Elisabeth Blazak had ever seen, and she was so taken with it that she became very involved in the sport. But the rent of the track was £300 per meeting, and it was very uneconomical, so we began to look for another venue. Mr Robert Bothway then offered us the track at Wreningham, and, with a lot of volunteer labour, all the running rails, fences, etc., were moved. And we now have the 'Ascot' of the harness racing world, because it is a beautifully maintained track, with a wonderful surface, and we race there every Thursday evening through the summer.'

John Hunt, Jason Ali, John Brincat, the Fairclough family and Mike Stutter all have good records at the track.

It is situated on the Wreningham road that runs north off the B1135, just west of B1113, eight miles south-west of Norwich.

Tregaron

Tregaron Trotting Club was formed in 1980 by a handful of Welsh locals who attended the Musselburgh Famous Pace and had a dream that they too could stage a meeting which would become as influential in the harness racing calendar. Each member put his hand in his pocket to donate £25 to make the dream materialize, and secretary, Gareth Lloyd Davies, was even more generous. Tregaron was at the time in the heart of 'flapping' (unaffiliated racing that is a mixed card of harness racing and 'galloping') country, so the original decision to stage a meeting affiliated to the BHRC was unquestionably a brave one. Aberystwyth-based architect, Peter Davies, was the inaugural chairman and remained at the head of things for twelve years, during which the dream was fully achieved – and then some – but not without a dire struggle in the beginning. Peter only relinquished the reins of the TTC to take the more significant position of chairman of Wales and the West Harness Racing Association in 1992. The current chairman is local butcher, Huw Evans, who has been a lifelong supporter of harness racing.

The first fixture that was intended to become a major one was held in 1980 on the Benjamin Brothers' Nantyderwen Farm between the Llandewi and Brefi villages and was a one-day mid-week meeting that attracted a mere twenty-six runners. The next couple of years were a similar story, and the committee who were working so hard to achieve their aim were becoming sadly disillusioned. At one of their regular meetings in a local pub, it was agreed that they change the venue to Doly-ry-chain Farm, owned by Mr and Mrs Glyn Davies, from where Peter Davies trained his horses at that time, close to the famous abbey estate, Strata Florida. Amalgamating three fields to make a superb half-mile grass track, the committee were still aware that the venue was geographically a backwater, and that a very real incentive would be needed to encourage owners to make the journey to the tiny Welsh village. Putting their hands in their pockets yet again, the members put up the prize money of a thousand pounds for the final, the first time such a lucrative offering had been made under the auspices of Wales and the West. Even then, things did not change dramatically overnight, and had it not been for the support of Staffordshire trainers Dave Taff and Stevie Lees, and stalwarts from Amman Valley, plus the locals, the success story would never have been.

That first prestigious Final in 1984 was indeed a poignant one due to the fact that it was won by Mountain Hero, driven by Teifion Thomas. The horse had been bred and formerly owned by the loyal inaugural secretary, Gareth Lloyd Davies, who had been taken ill at the meeting a year earlier and died of a heart complaint at his home a few hours later. The committee had donated a trophy for the Final in Gareth's memory, and it was an emotional moment indeed when his home-bred horse fought off the determined challenges of Billy Ocelot and Just A Joke to win his memorial race. Suddenly the imagination of the crowd was captured. What they witnessed at Tregaron was the sport's history in the making, and they vowed to be back for more. Nowdays the meeting boasts over 200 runners on its top class card, and a few years ago the numbers meant it had to become a two-day fixture on the Friday and Saturday of the last weekend in August. The legendary little stallion, Maradona, owned by local builder and trainer, Ronnie John, holds the track record of 2.5.4, set in the Free-for-All when he beat the brilliant McGuigan. 'And, though people find it hard to believe, we are pretty sure the track was one mile and eighteen yards that year because we had unwittingly put some posts further out on a bend than we should have, so it really was a remarkable performance,' observed Raymond Jenkins, who has been club secretary since 1984.

'Every Final (nowadays staged as an All Winners race) at Tregaron is breathtaking, the atmosphere is so special,' related Peter Davies, who has trained his own share of winners at the meeting, though so far, his dream of victory in the Final has eluded him. 'The Bousefields' stallion, Trew Seas, who won a couple of times was very popular with the crowd, and for me Stoneriggs JR and Colin Bevan winning both the Free-for-All and The Welsh Classic All Winners race in 1991 was outstanding. But Mountain Hero winning the first big Final was just as emotional, as was Extra Spring winning in 1993 for Clifford Dowse, driven by his son. Cliff is a local, and was with us right at the beginning, and put his hand in his pocket probably deeper than anyone when we had to find the big prize-money.'

In 1993, Extra Spring netted £3,000 for his narrow victory in the Final before a crowd of approximately 8,000, so progress has certainly been made. A fact that made his triumph all the sweeter is that Extra Spring only has the sight of one eye. As a youngster, he suffered a stable accident where his headcollar became caught, and the damage was caused by one of the metal buckles when he ran back in panic.

'Of course, it always has to be a good performance to win at Tregaron because we now attract the best runners in the country, but other victories that stick in my mind are Russian Square (1985), The Bounder (1987) and a horse called Lindy's Square who was handicapped off a hundred yards in the heat, that was before there was a maximum of eighty, and still won,' recalled Peter. Everyone has a special memory of Tregaron. For Raymond Jenkins, Huw Thomas's brilliant drive up the inner to take the Final with Hovis in 1990 was the most memorable victory, along with the local stal-

1993 Welsh Classic All Winners Race victor Extra Spring at Tregaron (blind eye side).

lion, Temple Star, winning the Free-for-All despite going to post as a rank outsider.

Luckily, several of the original supporters survived the initial doldrums. Mr Glyn Rees, who was the first President of the meeting, continues in that capacity, and the Llanybydder wholesale butcher, Oriel Jones, who was happy to provide a donation in those early days is also one of the main current sponsors.

The Tregaron Welsh Classic meeting was the first to secure television coverage from BBC and S4C, and acted as a catalyst for the live coverage which followed at Tir Prince. Stevie Lees is a consistently successful driver at the track, though Teifion Thomas is the only reinsman to have ever won the final on two occasions. The village becomes the object of pilgrimages by harness racing enthusiasts from all over Europe for that last weekend in August, and accommodation is best booked well in advance. Tregaron village was once described by one reveller as 'the outside of the Talbot Hotel' which is where the serious celebration and sympathizing is done.

9

Studs and Breeders

Though the English Thoroughbred is the foundation of the Standardbred breed, most of the fastest harness racehorses in the UK have had to resort to American influence on the bloodlines to improve their speed, even as long as a century ago.

At that time there were some famous trotters in Norfolk, who owed their performance to a great deal of Hackney blood, the foundation sire of this line being a stallion called Old Shales. He in turn went back to Flying Childers, who was the great, great grandsire of the magnificent Messenger. The most significant descendant of this Norfolk Hackney line was a stallion called Bellfounder, who was foaled in 1816 and was exported to America in 1822. Despite the fact that his dam was a mare of unknown pedigree, she was alleged to have trotted at 16 miles an hour on an English road. The major contribution that her son made to the breeding of the Standardbred was to sire the dam of the famous Hambletonian.

In the 1860s, progeny of Hambletonian began to set the 'trotting' scene alight in the USA. His sons, George Wilkes, Dictator, Happy Medium and Electioneer, were all to have a lasting effect on the breed, though it took time for this to be recognized. Peter the Great, by Happy Medium, was a natural pacer, and is the foundation of all of the prominent male lines of harness racehorses in America today.

Dictator sired a double-gaited horse (both pacing and trotting) called Direct, who was a brilliant performer himself, and in 1895 stood for a year at stud. His union with a mare called Bessie Hal resulted in a colt called Director Hal, who founded the line that gave us a world champion pacer, Billy Direct. This speedy performer sired Tar Heel, who was responsible for the speed in his own descendants, and is the sire of Sly Heel, the first stallion that Arthur Slack imported and stood at the Stoneriggs Stud in Cumbria in the early 1960s.

Even at the turn of this century, progressive spirits were racing horses that had been bred in the USA, mainly direct descendants of Peter the Great, or were using stallions such as Wellington Direct, an American import, on their own mares.

Speed has always been the all-important factor in the breeding of the Standardbred, and today the aim is just the same – a fast horse. Naturally, breeding stock must be of sound limb and powerful but athletic conformation, but slow horses win no prizes.

Because harness racing has been the Cinderella of racing for so many years, there are actually very few studs who produce Standardbreds commercially. On the other hand, almost everybody involved seems to have at least one mare tucked away somewhere, and race her progeny themselves, chasing the dream of having bred a classic winner.

Ian Drydale, who stands his stallions (currently the hugely successful pair, Fleet Decision and Armbro Mystic) at **Forest Mill** (see p. 15) in Scotland is acutely aware of the need for a premium scheme for the breed, perhaps along similar lines to the HIS (Hunter Improvement Society) scheme which so revolutionized the breeding of light horses in the UK. 'I try to keep my fees fairly low so that the working man with one good mare can afford to try and breed excellence,' he explained. In fact a plan to improve the breed and establish such a society is currently being examined by steward, Joe Hawkes, for the BHRC.

The sign outside the gate of the **Saunders Stud**, St Asaph, rural North Wales, proclaims that the owner, J. S. Jones, is the leading breeder of Standardbreds in the UK. Though JS, as he is widely known on the harness racing scene, is undoubtedly a man of vision, reliably reputed to be a millionaire and then some, even he cannot have anticipated the great success of the stud that he formed in 1964. Horses bearing the Saunders prefix are now famous worldwide and have won top races in USA, Australia, New Zealand, Canada, Germany and Zimbabwe as well as practically every classic in Britain.

JS has the golden touch, the kind of sharp business perception that cannot be instilled by education, and, though he started his working life milking cows for seven shillings a week, by the early 1960s he had flourishing businesses that included property-buying and farming. His first sight of harness racing was a visit to Prestatyn Raceway en route to his accountant, and he was exhilarated by the spectacle. He mentioned to his accountant that he would love to own a 'trotter', and the man agreed that it would be a very good idea to distract him from the stresses of his business life and encouraged him to go ahead.

'I paid 1,200 guineas for Enid Blyton,' announced JS triumphantly. 'Everyone thought I'd gone quite mad because it was a small fortune in those days. But you have to buy the best and hope for the best.' The golden touch was at work again, because she was one of the best brood mares of her time when her successful racing days were over. 'She even bred a foal at twenty-six years of age!' related JS.

Now in his eighties but showing little sign of physical frailty, he only relinquished his licence to drive in races a decade ago. His track debut was in fact a match at Prestatyn against Lord Langford, who was President of the BHRC from its inauguration until 1991 and was very influential in the progress of the sport. The prize was a crate of whisky, and JS lost. But, though it cost him a crate of whisky, he learned from the experience, and would never make the mistake of unbalancing his horse in a race again by being impatient.

The idea to breed Standardbreds evolved when JS was asked to quarantine 'transit' stallions which were being shipped from North America to Australia. He asked for two free services as payment from each classy animal liveried. Knowing that it is imperative to breed from good mares ('You can't *put* speed into 'em!'), JS imported some well bred, tough mares from New Zealand, Italy, Germany and the USA, and kept the best fillies that he produced. Thus began the mighty Saunders strain.

JS has stood many top-class stallions over the years, purchased on his annual 'shopping sprees' to the USA. Currently he owns the much sought-after Keystone Baron, who is by one of the most influential stallions in America, Most Happy Fella; Solitude by Tyler B ; Taurus Hanover, who stands in Dyfed with Ivor Davies, and Man About Town, who is with Ivan Brown in Cumbria.

Dorinda Birch organizes the twenty-odd brood mares and their offspring, and also does the breaking and training, always keeping JS high on the national winning owners table. Unquestionably, this shrewd man has had great influence on improving the breeding of Standardbred stock in the UK. 'Someone once told me, "You've been lucky, Mr Jones!" and I replied that he should put a "p" in front of it. I've been plucky! I've had one hell of a lot of worry with my horses over the years, but I've had a lot of fun, too!'

The **Stoneriggs Stud**, near Appleby, home of Arthur and Evelyn Slack, is another leading producer of top class Standardbred horses. The thousand-acre farm and breeding side of the set-up is Arthur's concern. Apart from the horses, he breeds Swaledale and Blue-Faced Leicester sheep, keeping in excess of 3,000 ewes. There are also 300 suckler cows.

Another winner for the Stoneriggs Stud. Evelyn Slack and Stoneriggs Inmate after winning the ladies race at Musselburgh in 1992.

Though Arthur is responsible for the buying of stallions, and the production of the world-famous Stoneriggs stock, he insists that all the credit for their outstanding successes on the track is down to the rest of his family, wife Evelyn, the trainer and driver, daughter Diane (Sayer) and son, Kenneth, both of whom have driven their share of winners. 'I don't interfere with them, and they don't interfere with me!' explained Arthur.

In 1993, the three-year-old colt, Stoneriggs Merc, won nine prestigious races, including the National Pacing Derby, and was voted BHRC Horse Of The Year. Arthur had earlier in the year sold a half-share in Merc to a colleague in the sheep-dealing world, Stephen Wood, who gifted it to his mother. Mrs Wood certainly never had cause to want to glance in Merc's mouth, since every time she attended the hitherto unknown races, he cruised to an impressive victory! Arthur Slack was unfamiliar with harness racing until he met Evelyn Hogarth, who converted him to her beloved sport, and he began to enjoy being a successful owner with his first horse in 1960, Millers Lad. 'He cost me eighty-two pounds,' recalled Arthur, 'I bought him fit, and had only had him ten days when we took him to Hawes Sports. Evelyn rode him, and I had ten pounds on him at 6–1, so when he won I felt I was really in business! Matt Miller was my next buy, and then one of my favourites, Dan Matthews. He won the Famous Musselburgh Pace the year we were married, 1962. He was a wonderful horse and won seventy-seven races for me.'

It was odds-on that Arthur would become interested in the breeding of harness racehorses due to his farming interests and it was while the Slacks were watching their horses race in Toronto that Arthur decided to import the stallion, Slyheel (USA). 'I bought him over, then got a few good mares together. Anyone can *buy* success, it's much more satisfying to *breed* it.'

Arthur was also responsible for importing the stallions Armbro Mystic (Can.) – who is not only a sire of good winners, but also well established as a brood mare sire – HT Navy and Fleet Decision, who is the current leading sire of winners in the UK.

The brilliant mare, Monkroyd Mystery, by HT Navy, won fifty-two races in three seasons for the Slacks before retiring to the paddocks. Arthur emphasizes how very important the 'bottom (maternal) line' is to breed for performance, and is looking forward to seeing Monkroyd Mystery's offspring on the track.

All breeders are ultimately aiming to produce champions, and the Stoneriggs Stud have certainly bred their quota since being formed in the 1960s. Merc's half-brother, Stoneriggs G'Patron and Stoneriggs Kid are only two of the tough horses now winning in the States in tremendous times, and in 1991 three out of the four Sires Stakes Classic finals were won by Stoneriggs horses.

The whole Slack family is involved with their horses, and they all say that to have bred a horse which gets to the wire first gives that triumph a very special significance. To consistently breed such high-class horses from only half a dozen or so mares is more than a triumph, and it is certainly a tribute to the thoroughness that Arthur Slack applies to his 'interest'.

Nora Cole's **Golden Future** stud at Seisdon, near Wolverhampton, also has a good reputation. It was established in the early 1970s by Nora and her late husband, Ted, and was largely put on the map by the brilliant stallion, Ted's Choice. He was imported from America by Nora's father-in-law, and was originally called Golden Future. The bay horse had an outstanding race career in this country, regularly recording 2 minutes,

6 seconds off a big handicap at Prestatyn, and on one occasion at Manchester, fell in a race, regained his feet and still won. Ted's Choice died peacefully at his home, among friends, in the early 1990s, having attained a great age and left many offspring to maintain the memory of a great horse.

Raceover is another stallion at the Golden Future Stud who has devotees, and he is proving to be a valuable brood mare sire. Skippers Subject and Whitehall General are also available at Seisdon.

'I didn't used to be completely convinced, but I've come to the conclusion that the mare is the most important factor. There are undoubtedly some who will breed winners no matter what you put them to, like my own Velvet Harmony,' disclosed Nora.

The stud naturally produces youngsters for sale, though the best fillies are kept, and Nora specializes in producing two-year-olds to race. The first two home in the 1993 two-year-old fillies Sires Stakes were the progeny of the Golden Future Stud.

The Maw family, from near Sunderland, stand the American import, Surfer Hanover (by No Nukes) at **Coalford Lane Farm** and have fifteen good mares. Believing the maternal line to be vital in producing performance stock, Gary Maw has spent much time in America, studying the breeding policies over there, and has imported some classy, fast mares. He believes that this is vital to achieve the best possible bloodlines. 'The breeding in America is fifteen or twenty years ahead of us, and the difference is that over there it is a thriving industry, and they are having to breed for a commercial market. This makes everything very competitive, so the breeder has to be especially selective. Only the top three or four stallions are owned by syndicates, and the new stallions are offered at introductory fees. If they don't have a successful first crop, the stud fee drops dramatically; a poor second crop, and they get shipped out of the country.

'In my opinion, a well bred stallion should also have a good race record too, and the best thing that happened to the breeding of the British Standardbred was the blood introduced by the transit stallions that were quarantined with people like Sam Ballantyne and JS Jones. They were tough, well bred individuals and had all raced well, but breeders need to use a strong maternal line as well. In America, though Albatross and Niatross were brilliant horses, they are not particularly good sires of sires, most of the sons have failed at stud. But they are more successful in the maternal line. The stallions that have had the most influence on breeding in the USA are Abercrombie, Most Happy Fella,

No Nukes and Cam Fella. And of course it is big business over there, good horses can win millions of dollars.

'Hopefully now the sport will go forward, and the demand for stock will increase,' prophesied Gary with optimism. Having already bred such good horses as Stepaway (by Keystone Baron) and Overdrive (by Raceover), Gary Maw is now hoping for even greater things.

Gary Maw is not alone in his beliefs that we have to look to the USA to improve bloodlines. **Brian Davies**, from near Sennybridge, flew out to America in 1992 to select a stallion in an effort to improve the choice of Standardbred sires in South Wales, and purchased Master Scoot, by Matt's Scooter. Brian too, imported a mare, to strengthen the American influence on the maternal line of his stock. The British breeder now not only has the choice of established and successful sires with whom he is familiar, but there are several American imports to choose from such as Disraeli Hanover, Control Factor, Sunbeam, Handsome Sum, Prince Lee Dancer, and Burst Of Energy to name but a few other than the ones already mentioned.

Brian Davies's imported stallion Master Scoot (USA) by Matt's Scooter (USA).

UK mile record-holder, Golden Dale, with Alan Haythornthwaite, 1.59.4.

Golden Dale's UK mile record of 1.59.4 set in 1992 at York with Alan Haythornthwaite will soon be under strong fire. The world mile record is constantly changing in America by fractions of a second, but is just over 1 minute, 46 seconds, so British-bred stock has some headway to make in the speed department. The British are not obsessed with speed and records, which can turn racing into a procession rather than a blood-stirring spectacle – winning tends to be the important thing. But with the ever-improving introduction of new bloodlines, soon they will be required to pace faster to the winners' circle.

10

BHRC and Associations

Though harness racing had been healthy in localized areas around the UK since the turn of the century, there was no standardization of handicapping or rules. Each track had its own system, and each one was different. If a horse or driver managed to transgress the rules and be suspended from competing on one circuit, there was little to stop him merely racing at another. A ruling body for the sport was badly needed, and when the New Zealander, Noel Simpson, built Prestatyn Raceway in the early 1960s, it acted as a catalyst for the formation of an association that would control and discipline the sport.

Six people were responsible for the new enterprise at Prestatyn: brothers Noel and William Simpson, William and Kelvin White, Arthur Massey and Lord Langford. The raceway was officially opened on Friday, July 26th, 1963, by Billy Butlin, OBE, and he did not restrict himself to tamely cutting a ribbon and making a speech. Instead, he pulled on the compulsory white overalls and drove a match with Lord Langford to declare the £150,000 stadium open.

The directors of the raceway formed the Night Trotting Co. Ltd, who endeavoured to run racing there on the highest possible level, and only accepted horses and trainers registered with them, plus Continental pacers, to contest their events. Over a thousand pounds in prize money was on offer for the inaugural meeting, and the first race was won by Outlaw, driven by his owner, Mr Lipton of Maidenhead, who had been converted to the sport from flat racing. The rules of the raceway were strictly enforced by the body of stewards, of which Lord Langford was chairman, and Bill Simpson was

Action in Wales and the West. Elaine Stillwell and Pinnochio lead Nijinsky, the 'grey wonder' (Mike Stutter), at Upton-on-Severn.

appointed as handicapper. The company produced a rule book, which was a compulsory purchase, costing two shillings for members. All this was a gigantic step in the right direction for the sport.

In 1964, the United Kingdom Trotting Association was formed by several of the owners of horses that raced at Prestatyn, with Wing Commander Cowden and Lord Langford at the helm. Mrs Mylon and Mavis Smart were the first joint secretaries, and put in an incredible amount of hard work to produce the UK's first Standardbred Stud book, and the first record book in 1965. It became even more obvious to the organizers of racing at Prestatyn that control of the sport at a national level was vital, but the UKTA did not feel the time was right for them to assume command, and the National Harness Racing Club was formed as the ruling body. In 1969, it was announced that the NHRC was fully functional and would operate for harness racing along the same lines as the Jockey Club did for its Thoroughbred counterpart. Six tracks were affiliated to the NHRC at that time, including Musselburgh. Lord Langford was the inaugural president, and with the tireless Megan Royle as his secretary, worked constantly to promote and improve the sport that was so close to his heart. Despite the fact that Mrs Royle had no previous connections with harness racing, she was intensely interested in her work and played a major part in the original organization of licensing members and their horses. Since the 'National' in the title of the club was slightly ambiguous, it was amended to the British Harness Racing Club.

Mavis Smart and her husband, Stan, who were based in Chesterfield, were key figures in tabulating and recording pedigrees, an important foundation on which breeders of Standardbred horses would build.

All the people involved in these associations at this time, or indeed at any time, have done an amazing amount of painstaking work to produce records and stud books so that the sport would at last know where it was going. Today the title of the UKTA has been amended to use the description 'Harness Racing' rather than the outmoded term 'Trotting', and is now known as UKHRA. Elizabeth Towe, who is the daughter of legendary driver Clem Dodd, is the busy secretary.

Anne Brophy, who is the current 'backbone' of the British Harness Racing Club, carried on the stirling work where Megan Royle left off in 1983. Anne has always been involved in the equestrian world, but her introduction to harness racing was a visit to Prestatyn Raceway in 1963. She was captivated, and, living locally, came as a spectator regularly. Her 'hands on' involvement came between 1966–70, when she was employed at the stadium as a marshal. Unfortunately, the raceway then suffered the same fate as many did at that time and was sold for development. Prestatyn in fact became one of Fred Pontin's holiday camps. Between 1970 and 1975, Anne's harness racing activities were restricted to forays to the busy circuits at Kendal, Chasewater (Staffordshire) and Droylsden (one of the Manchester tracks) to watch occasionally, but she became completely hooked in 1975 when approached by a local farmer, Arthur Wright, the owner of the class New Zealand mare, Glenila. 'I was asked to help break two-year-olds for the track, and we raced them (we even trained winners!) mostly at Droylsden, but occasionally at Kendal. They were invariably sold at the end of the racing season, and most went on to be very successful. Stayila, Bye Bye Glen, Canila and Pessida were all exported to the USA and Canada,' recalled Anne.

'Then time went on, and I suppose I just got fed up of breaking fingers and all the drawbacks of educating youngsters! From 1982–86, I was involved with the North Wales Harness Racing Club, promoting racing on grass circuits at Talacre, Llanerch Park and St Asaph. In 1983, I was offered the position as National Secretary and thought how nice it would be to work from home . . .!' Nowdays Anne is kept fully occupied with all the documentation connected with BHRC and only has two old ponies in her stables, but makes time to spectate at Tir Prince Raceway whenever possible.

Scotsman Tom Menzies has been Chairman of BHRC since 1982. A successful owner and trainer, having been responsible for seven winners in 1993, Mr Menzies has always been interested in harness racing due to the involvement of his brother, John, who was a leading rider in Scotland, contesting the 'trotting' races at such venues as the Highland Games. His own passion was amateur boxing, and, during his military service between 1960–64, he became the British Army and Imperial Services Boxing Champion. Not that the honours were going to stop there, for he was chosen to represent Scotland at The British Empire and Commonwealth Games in Australia. 'I was so pleased at being selected, I felt as if I'd been crowned King!' he smiled, and, strangely, it was this journey to the Antipodes that was to be the catalyst to his greater involvement in harness racing. The competitors in the games were accommodated in the homes of expatriated British folks, and Tom was taken by his hosts to view a harness racing meeting at Gloucester Park Raceway in Perth, Western Australia.

He was inspired by the experience. 'It was like attending Royal Ascot in comparison to the fixtures we had at home, and I couldn't help wondering why we couldn't have that sort of set-up in the United Kingdom.' On his return to Scotland, he purchased Pirnielodge Princess, who was to be the foundation mare of all his winning stock, and nowadays the whole Menzies family is involved; his sons, Hugh and Kenneth, and nephew Gregor are all excellent drivers. 'In 1975 I won the Three Year-Old Championship at

Droylsden with Almondell Clansman, worth £500. I built a block of stables with the prize money! It seemed to go further then!'

Tom Menzies strongly believes that harness racing needs to be affiliated to the British Horseracing Board/Jockey Club for its image to become totally acceptable.

At the AGM of the BHRC in 1992, Lord Langford, who had worked ceaselessly to further the sport of harness racing, decided that his approaching 80th birthday was a good enough reason to retire as President. The position was offered to his Vice-President, His Honour Sir Sanderson Temple, MBE, QC, who graciously accepted.

Eden Valley Trotting Association

Currently, eighteen meetings in the north of England are held under the auspices of the Eden Valley Trotting Association, including the four held at Appleby. George Coward is President of the Association in 1994, and he and his son, Les, have been ardent supporters of harness racing in the area. The association was originally named the Eden Valley and District Pony Racing Association, because directly after the War there were as many 'galloping' events as 'trotting' in the area. The original objective of the EVDPRA, which was founded in 1946, has remained largely unchanged – to assist promoters of horse events and provide the necessary officials to enforce the relevant handicaps and racecourse rules. Each organizer wishing to run under the auspices of the association paid an affiliation fee, and all owners had to register their horses with the association to be eligible to race.

The initial committee was chaired by Mr T. Bainbridge, with Mr J. L. Harker as Secretary/Treasurer, the rest comprising promoters, owners, delegates and various race officials such as starters, handicappers and stewards. In 1950, Mr T. Ellwood was made the inaugural President. During that first year, there were twenty affiliations, covering the counties of Cumberland and Westmorland, North Yorkshire and the Durham borders. Most of these events were supporting programmes to foot races, or grass track motorcycle racing. The early 1950s saw an explosion in the number of trotters and pacers in the area, and the title of the association was altered to include the word 'Trotting'. Two separate handicapping panels were formed to apply to driving and riding. The popularity of the sport increased greatly during that decade. Trotting races were generally run as mixed events, with horses either in the sulky or under saddle, but as entries were abundant, promoters began to frame separate heats and final handicaps for each class.

By 1959, harness racing was still very healthy, but pony racing was on the wane, necessitating another change in the title of the body, which became Eden Valley and District Trotting and Galloping Association. During this year, registration of horses improved, and all jockeys and drivers were also required to be registered, using the format currently used by the BHRC.

When the NHRC was formed in the early 1960s, Eden Valley became a founder member. All galloping races were dropped from their events, and since all connections needed to register nationally, their own scheme ceased. The title was finally changed to what it is today.

The EVTA still strictly officiated over its meetings, and in 1982 introduced video equipment to assist judges and stewards, and in 1984, evolved a handicap system which created much less discontent amongst the horse owners. The EVTA has always restricted its jurisdiction to grass circuits, and officiated at Kendal for five years until the opening of its hard track in 1972, and likewise at York until the hard track was built in 1978.

Loyalty is obviously very strong in the EVTA, with numerous officials giving up their time for their sport, travelling to distant venues. During the life of the association there have only been only four secretaries and three treasurers, which speaks of the true commitment to the sport in the north of England.

'It's interesting to note the increase in prize money that has been offered in the region over the years,' observed Les Coward. 'In 1973 there were 24 fixtures for a total of £7,000 prize money; in 1983, 21 meetings for £22,000, and in 1993, 17 fixtures for no less than £77,000.' In 1993, Mike Lord was champion driver in the area, with Jim McInally just behind him. Heroine of the 1993 Appleby Spring Meeting, Helen Morton, was the leading lady driver, but Diane Bousefield took the Ladies Championship for the most points accumulated in heats and finals. Jim Winter was the leading trainer from Charlie Kirk, and top horse in the region was Mr J. Blaylock's Denton Lee. The best all round turnout over the season was adjudged to be George McGregor's Mattie Lobell.

Wales and the West Harness Racing Association

Wales and the West Harness Racing Association is the promoter of twenty-two meetings on grass. Though this area is often referred to as 'Wales', the tracks are mainly on the Welsh borders in Herefordshire, but extend to Worcestershire and Gloucestershire, with only a handful actually in Wales, though these include the mighty Tregaron. One meeting is also held in the south-west annually by Devon and Cornwall Trotting Club.

This is the only region of the country where unaffiliated harness racing occurs, run by the Mid-Wales Association and widely referred to as 'flapping'. Though this racing is unrecognized by the BHRC, an amnesty was offered by Lord Langford in 1979/80 to attract connections to compete

Steve Flook, leading trainer in Wales and the West, with Rozanante at Walton, from Carl Davies, Tom Harper and Dave Taff.

under the 'legal' code. Many seized the opportunity, knowing this was the only direction in which they could really achieve anything, since the better circuits with the superior prize-money were all for affiliated horses, and the stock bred by 'flapping' men was not eligible for registration in the stud book, thus limiting their market. Though many people apply to be accepted under BHRC rules from the Mid-Wales (unaffiliated) Association yearly, there is still a certain amount of friction between the two sides, who both believe 'their' racing is best.

WWHRA was formed in 1980, as a direct result of the amnesty, with a view to improving the sport, and fifty members joined immediately. There are currently almost three hundred members, which make up 23% of the membership of BHRC.

Peter Davies took the chair in 1991/2 and is 'determined to drag the sport out of the 1960s'. He has formed an executive committee which is promoting and marketing the sport, an extremely positive move. 'We have a valuable commodity in harness racing,' stated Peter firmly, 'but it is poorly marketed and run by part-timers.'

Official WWHRA track measurer, Roy Pugh, is a whizz with mathematics and statistics, and compiled the following for the 1993 season: 18 fixtures were held in Wales and the West, with 172 races run for a total of £52,235; 319 different horses contested the events to make 1,342 starters; 146 horses won or were placed, one of these being Stoneriggs Herbie, who made the most appearances in the region, going to post on 21 occasions.

The fastest mile rate of the season in the area was recorded by Ronnie John's brilliant mare, Disco Dazzler, at the Tregaron spring meeting, where she clocked a sizzling 2.07.3. Tragically, she died of colic later in the year, a great loss.

The top driver of Wales and the West was Roy Wilson, from Llandrindod Wells, who won twenty-one races in only his second season under BHRC rules. This was one more than Steve Flook, who reaped consolation by taking the Leading Trainer award. Steve is one of the best-known figures on the circuits of Wales and the West, and his outstanding success is a tribute to his dogged resilience. His career with horses began when he was apprenticed as a teenager to flat trainer, Arthur Pitt, but he swapped to being a National Hunt jockey when increasing weight began to be a problem. Steve's great promise 'over the sticks' was cut painfully short by a bone-splintering fall in a Wincanton hurdle race which left surgeons muttering darkly that he would never ride again. His horrendous injuries included a fractured femur which had to be surgically fixed with a K-Nail, which runs inside the length of the thighbone. With typical stubbornness, Steve proved the doctors wrong, but was forced to retire from his career as a jockey. He was introduced to harness racing by trainer, Bill Morris, who made a chance remark in a pub that he could not find a driver for his string. After sampling the excitements of the sulky seat on the training grounds, Steve passed the compulsory test and went on to win on his race debut at Amman Valley with Double Deal. Since then he has consistently taken various championships in the area, including the most victories with one horse in the region in 1993, scoring seven times with Peter Kendrick's Rozanante.

The WWHRA leading owner of 1993 was Tom Harper, who had ten wins with only two horses. Luck was certainly on Tom's side, because he only purchased Charmagres Gold in August from Maidenhead trainer, Roy Willis, when his prolific winner, Saunders Premier, knocked himself. Charmagres Gold went on to become the second-highest winner of prize money in the locality, behind Tregaron hero, Extra Spring.

Leading owner-driver was newcomer Dai Langford with Wrekin Ron Lobell, who was the horse most consistently winning or placed in 1993.

The current WWHRA secretary is the tireless and dedicated Heulwen Thomas, who not only juggles the administration of the association with her demanding job in the National Library of Wales, but also assists Henry Bulman in his success as a trainer and driver. She was unwittingly nominated

Tom Harper's Charmagres Gold and Gary Wakefield winning the £1,000 final at Broadheath. He was one of the top money-winners in Wales and the West.

for the position as WWHRA secretary in 1991 and has been efficiently installed ever since. The treasurer is Magaret Langford, whose husband Jeff is a well established trainer at Hundred House. Both Jeff and daughter Helen drive their quota of winners. The stalwart, Fred Bufton and Tregaron man, Raymond Jenkins, are the official race-secretaries of the area, and Laura Beddis and Derek James officiate at the fixtures as BHRC stewards. Ex-jockey Alf Launchbury has the distinction of being elected as the first Safety Officer for the Association.

The British Harness Racecourse Association

This was originally formed in 1991/2 as the Hard Track Association, mainly to represent the raceways during negotiations of the BHRC with the Jockey Club. Mainstays of the operation are Billy Williams, Barry Delaney and Richard Muddle, and, early in 1993, the title was changed so that grass circuits could be included. The aims of the BHRA are to represent the best interests of their members with any future negotiations with the British Horseracing Board and to promote the sport of harness racing.

A recent development has been the formation of a Grass Track Association, so that all the grass circuits, including the small independents, are united under one flag.

The Scottish Trotting Horse Owners Association

This was formed in 1929 to promote meetings in Scotland. The first fixture was held at Kilmarnock on April 17th that year, attracting twenty-nine horses, all under saddle: the final was won by Mr T. Foster's mare, Little Sylvia. This was one of forty meetings that were under the jurisdiction of the STHOA at that time.

There were over thirty members of the association then, which drew up a set of rules which were strictly applied to the meetings. This included a start behind tapes, where horses faced the opposite way until a signal was given to turn and a pistol fired from the start-line. The initial handicapper was Ralf Reid, the first judge was Adam Arnot and William Fyfe was the original secretary. Over the years, Mrs Isa Walker of the Riverbank Stables has been a tower of strength in this association, producing a *Trotting* magazine and inexhaustably promoting meetings to enable the sport to make a multitude of donations to deserving charities.

The current, very active chairman is John McCormack, and Alistair Smith, who is reputed to be 'the one man in harness racing who has never had anything bad said about him!' is secretary. Nowadays the STHOA boasts in excess of a hundred members, but does not promote meetings in Scotland as each fixture is run independently.

There are a handful of other associations in the harness racing world: The Professional Trainers And Drivers Association, The Harness Horse Owners Association and The North East Standardbred Association included.

Unfortunately, since the lease expired on the Antrim Stadium, there is no recognized circuit in Northern Ireland. Many registered owners travel their horses to the mainland to race at Corbiewood and Tir Prince, and record their share of successes at the tracks.

As well as the various associations, there are numerous thriving harness racing clubs all over the country who meet regularly and organize fixtures, indulging their habit of discussing horses and harness racing at the slightest excuse! But it is only recently that these enthusiasts have begun to realize that they should be trying to promote themselves beyond their own followers and that there is a whole country of potential supporters out there who know next to nothing about harness racing through no fault of their own!

Having at last captured the imagination of the media, and with the advent of Dunstall Park, all that is now changing . . . watch this space!

11

Classic Characters of the Circuits

The horse world in general is crawling with characters, and the harness racing scene is no exception. Whatever their role in the scheme of things (many have already been mentioned in the text) they all love their sport dearly. And it is odds-on that none of them do it for the money.

THE HORSES

The stirring sight of top-class horses battling courageously from the gate in a Free-for-All, a sizzling mêlée of power and speed, inspires an elation that defies description. The sheer guts of these brilliant horses, their refusal to accept defeat, would be their downfall if they were run consistently in handicaps, since giving newly upgraded fast horses 80 yards start over them is often too much to ask, and such is their will to win that it breaks their hearts to be beaten off a maximum deficit. Consequently the best horses run in races with no handicap, they all start on equal terms off the gate, and the fastest horse on the day wins.

When **Golden Dale** (San San Almahurst (USA)/Dancing Dale), who is currently the quickest harness racehorse in the country, is on form, his burst of acceleration is nothing short of breathtaking. Owned by Jack Gissing, and trained by his son-in-law, Clifford Haythornthwaite, the tough bay is known as 'Bill' (after Bill Sowerby, his breeder) at home. Watching him in action, his long, low stride floating over the ground, he is an imposing sight, and it is a shock to find he is only a little over 15 h.h. He adores his racing, and is not broken to saddle, so does all his work in the cart, and Clifford (who 'practically lives with him') often jogs him around the farm tracks and lanes. But such is Bill's fanaticism for racing that Clifford has to

Top-class Free-for-All winner Kohima with Alan Udale.

be constantly on his guard for anyone on a bicycle, or Bill is instantly in competitive mode, and shifts up through the gears very smartly to take them on! Bill does not suffer fools gladly, and, though he would not actually hurt anyone, he has given a few people severe shocks with his habit of rushing at the stable door pulling a highly ferocious face. Golden Dale was voted BHRC Horse Of The Year in 1991, and celebrated by breaking his own UK mile record at York in 1992 on his first outing, to the surprise of his connections, as he had started his campaign late due to a virus.

Kohima (Rajah Lobell (USA)/Kevock Blue) is another truly exciting performer. Alan Udale drove him in the early 1990s to devastate class fields with his turn of foot from the last turn, coming from last to first in seconds. Stuart Sowerby also piloted him using quite different tactics, and the result was the same, the black (technically dark bay!) horse scorching to the wire in only a little over the two minute barrier.

The Danish-bred **Nijinsky** (Osman Bogo/Cerina Ostrup), the 'grey wonder', actually has the pedigree of a square trotter, but was pretty moderate in his diagonally gaited races. He was sold for a song to his current driver, Mike Stutter, and it was only by accident that Mike and the late

Peter Gray's Nijinsky, favourite with the crowd, driven by Mike Stutter.

trainer, Alfie Bates, discovered that he paced. They furnished him with hopples, and he never looked back, pacing from maiden to open handicap company in his first season, only being beaten twice. A top-class performer, the beautiful stallion is every inch the stuff that fairy tales are made of, and nowadays belongs to Peter Gray.

Jimmy's Decision (Fleet Decision (USA)/Bright Wire) was another top three-year-old in 1993, and his string of victories ensured that he was made a hot favourite for the National Pacing Derby, where he suffered defeat by another outstanding animal, **Stoneriggs Merc** (Fleet Decision (USA)/Wheatley Patron). John Mac, who owns Jimmy's Decision, is a great supporter of the sport and enjoys racing himself on the grass circuits of Wales and the West during the summer, mainly educating youngsters in the novice grades. He happened to see an advertisement in the *Farmers Guardian* for a couple of Standardbred horses and went to view them. Liking what he saw, he did the deal, and sent the colt, who had been a useful two-year-old, to Stevie Lees to train. When John rang to ask how the horse was going some time later, Stevie told him that the colt was much too good to waste and requested that he could keep him to race. 'When my wife, Carol, and I went to watch him working, we couldn't believe it!' declared John. Indeed

Crack colt, Jimmy's Decision, on his way to victory at Tir Prince Raceway with Steve Lees.

the colt, who had appeared almost invincible prior to the Derby, recorded a time very close to two minutes at York, and unofficially did break the two-minute barrier in a workout.

Outlaw (Teddy Butler (USA)/Moonshine) is the only horse that is owned and trained by Sennybridge agricultural contractor, Wesley Jones. As tough as they come, the stallion powered home to take the 1992 Welsh Classic All Winners Race at Tregaron (see cover picture) at ten years of age, a 'catch' (spare) drive for Alan Haythornthwaite. The following year saw Outlaw have the most amazing campaign; the more that was asked of him, the more he gave. He won five top-class races in a week, one of which was an International Free-for-All at Tir Prince, where an extended distance saw him take the scalp of Golden Dale when driven by Roy Wilson. The previous day he had won the biggest handicap final of the season at Amman Valley, the Barclays Bank Challenge Trophy with Wesley, his owner. Four days later he recorded the fastest mile-rate of the day when taking the top-graded race at Allensmore.

McGuigan (Rajah Lobell (USA)/Corinne Adios) and **Armbro Fling** (Armbro Mystic (Can.)/Sly Solar) are both track-record holders, while **Red Admiral** (Truba Rainbow (USA)/Adelina), the 'iron horse' **Stepaway**

(Keystone Baron (USA)/Cool Streak), Mike Lord's favourite, **Saunders Destiny**, **Ronald's Gold** (Kerry Gold (USA)/Jaqueline Byrd) and **Surprise Skipper** (Flight Messenger (USA)/Lagonda) all win their share of important races. Swale Forrest's superb mare, **Denton Cover** (Cover Up (USA)/Denton Patsy) is surely poised for great things, having been unlucky enough to suffer a fall at Musselburgh in 1993, and **Stoneriggs JR** (Rajah Lobell (USA)/Stoneriggs Dixie) disproves the theory that a horse cannot handle two jobs by combining his stud duties with scorching appearances on the circuits. The grand veterans, **Granell Rhapsody** (Dixieland (USA)/March Brown) and **Soldier Boy** (Slyheel (USA)/Suzy Sota) are still dour battlers and should never be written off. And every year there is the next crop of potential champions appearing, chasing the hopes and dreams of their owners, some of whom will eventually join the exclusive ranks of the Free-for-All contenders, their performances written in the record books and indelibly etched on the memories of the spectators.

There have been some very exceptional harness racehorses in the past. In 1929, **Golden Dollar**, a son of Chestnut Peter (by Peter the Great), paced a mile and 100 yards at Audenshaw in 2.13½. This was a handicap record and the gelding went on to win many top events, bettering this time a few weeks later at Greenford Park. Trained by Jim Booth, the American import was owned by the well known Blackpool millionnaire, Charles Smith.

The roan trotting gelding, **Herbie M,** raced with great success at Greenford Park between 1921–23, setting a mile record there of 2.23 before he was sold to race in Belgium, where his victories continued.

Dixie Direct, **Teddy's Wee Sister**, **Saxon Queen II**, **Dan Direct** and **Call Boy** were all very fast pacers in the 1920s and 1930s, the latter incredibly setting race records as a yearling, a two-year-old and a three-year-old. One of the most stirring performers of that time was **Rosetta M**. The American-bred granddaughter of Peter the Great was without a doubt the darling of the circuits, for she was not only the fastest trotting mare around, consistently winning Championship 'long' mile races at a rate of 2.16, but she was stone blind. Rosetta M was always jogged slowly for a couple of circuits as a warm-up to get the 'feel' of it, then in the actual race would rely entirely on her driver's judgement, scorching home in blistering times. Phyllis James remembers her when she was trained by her father, Bill Evans. 'She really was completely blind, the most amazing mare! She could never be turned out because she had to be familiar with her surroundings.' The 'grand trotting mare' who regularly made headlines, and aroused such emotion with the crowds, was also trained with great success by Jack Lewzey and M. Marks.

BHRC national drivers champion, Mike Lord.

THE PEOPLE

Mike Lord

Having driven his first winner, Jack Laing's Scottish Son, in his debut at the age of fifteen, Mike knew he would always be happiest when piloting racehorses around the circuits. Winner of his first National Championship in 1992, Mike has driven in France, Belgium and Germany, but claims that it makes no difference to him which country he is competing in, or whether it's a trotter or a pacer in front of him, it's the racing that is important. 'It doesn't matter to me whether it's Florida or Hawes, it's being behind a horse that counts.'

Chairman of the Professional Trainer and Drivers Association, he is keen to see the sport go forward so that the professional can earn a decent living at it, but without leaving the 'small men' behind. 'A lot of folks know just what is needed to take the sport on, but they're afraid to hand over the reins in case they lose control of what they see as "their" sport. They can't seem to realize that they are the "grassroots" of it, and that no matter how many new people come in, they have the advantage of sound basic knowledge. They should thrive on competition. Not fear it.' It is certainly difficult to be a professional as a driver, since there is no realistic official fee laid down for the service. Mike, who drives for top trainers such as Granville Ainley, Jim Winter and John Gill, keeps the peace when he has divided loyalties by always choosing the horse he considers has the best chance to win. This method is accepted by owners and trainers alike, so that no-one can be offended, and, as Mike is only human, he has been known to get it wrong! There is also no official provision made for collection of driving fees, which makes life even more difficult for the professional. 'They only don't pay once, I never drive for them again if I have trouble,' Mike smiled, now in the happy position of having plenty of horses to choose from.

Despite his polite and charming exterior, there is a glint of fanaticism in Mike Lord's eye that suggests that being the best is very important to him. He admits it. 'I've always liked winning better than losing. I used to be a very bad loser, but I've got a bit older now!' He has won practically every British Classic, including the 1985 National Pacing Derby with Barry Delaney's Saunders Computer, the 1986 Two-Year-old Futurity with Unique and the Sires Stakes with Saunders Destiny, McGuigan and Harriet Lobell.

The odd painful injury has been the 'downside' for Mike, with cracked ribs and a ruptured tendon sheath, contracted when a horse behind 'climbed' over the top of him. He has long been an advocate of the body-protector, and feels things could have been much more serious without his. 'I've worn one for years,' he smiled. 'The other drivers used to gently pull my leg about it, then they've had a bang themselves and decided I'm not so daft after all . . .' Currently based near York, Mike covers hundreds of miles a season to contest almost twice as many races as any other driver on the circuits. 'It's my job!' he conceded, adding, 'But I don't traipse up and down the country to get beat! Of course sometimes I do, but I don't leave home with that possibility in mind!'

Stevie Lees

Stevie is a respected international driver, having driven winners in eight different countries. Small and dynamic, he is an unnerving person to be around, on or off the track, and his talent and his complete belief in his own ability have occasionally alienated his opponents. Stevie is unworried by such trivialities and concentrates on one of the most important aims in his particular scheme of things, getting to the wire in front. A top professional, he does not dismiss driving as 'just a job' and agrees that he gets a buzz from it, but a bigger one from winning.

The Lees family have long been connected with harness racing, but Stevie was largely unmoved by it in his youth, preferring to compete at shows on his gymkhana ponies. However, in his teens, he developed the 'need for speed' and turned his attentions to trotters and pacers. Leebro Adios provided his first winner at Chasewater Raceway when Stevie was sixteen years of age, and he has been both National Champion Driver and Trainer several times since. Because of his size, it was often suggested that perhaps he would have made it as a jockey. This is guaranteed to make Stevie bristle. 'I *am* a jockey!' he replied testily. 'I just sit in a different place! The judgement of pace and timing are just the same . . .'

Stevie often spends the winter driving in Florida, where he has been in the top ten per cent of trainers. Stevie enjoys Florida because the prize-money is more realistic, and the races are better framed, so that different levels of competition give more horses a chance of winning. 'Not everyone can own a top-class horse,' he points out, 'but the others cost just the same to keep.' Also, the driving is much more clear cut; if you clash wheels with someone, you are banned. 'It's a bit like going back to school when you first drive over there, everything is so much faster. And the faster you drive, the faster you have to think . . .' He has recorded the blistering time of 1.54 in Florida, and over here has officially clocked two minutes with the great mare Black and Silver. His favourite horse was Donnisthorpe King, who won his last eleven starts and broke five track records as a three-year-old. But Saunders Roman, who provided him with eighteen victories in one season, is another who was recalled with affection. Having said that, Stevie does not believe in making pets of his horses, many of whom are trained by his uncle, Paul, the current Champion Trainer, from his yard in Lichfield. 'They have the best of everything, which is how it should be.'

Stevie Lees calculates that he covers 350 miles weekly on the jogging cart alone, without his race drives and their corresponding warm-ups.

In 1992 he married Alex, who is also a more-than-capable pilot, and despite only having recently given birth to a son, she took the 1993 Musselburgh Ladies Race with Howard's Way. Marriage may have softened Stevie Lees' character, but it has not made him any less formidable as an opponent on the circuits. Having won almost every major British Classic, he also holds two national speed records with the trotters, Ghandy's Chance and Ideal Key.

Alan Haythornthwaite

The Haythornthwaite yard, on the borders of Lancashire and Yorkshire, is very much a family affair. Alan's brother, Clifford, is the trainer, and his sister, Pam, is also a well respected driver. Theresa, Alan's wife, also does her share, along with caring for their brace of sons. Thus the triumphs of the half a dozen or so horses that are raced from there, including the mighty Golden Dale, are always fully appreciated. Alan Haythornthwaite is so far the only man to have clocked under the two minute mile on the circuits of Great Britain, and he has done so on three occasions, once with Missing Link, and twice with Golden Dale. This feat means much to the pleasantly cheerful 'nice guy' of harness racing.

Alan was first interested in the sport as a boy, when he accompanied his father as a spectator. 'I wanted to be a jockey in those days and my father told me not to be so daft, I was to get a proper job. When I was nineteen, I was doing a milk round, and bought myself a pacer caller Flamingo's Pride. Father went absolutely mad! Mind you, he was the first one who wanted to be there when we took him to the races! We finished fourth at Kendal on our first run, then third, then we won! Then I fell off . . . ! But we won six races with that horse before we sold him on, and Clifford and I have been in partnership ever since.'

It is quite obvious that Alan is terminally obsessed with harness racing and that he finds each victory a real triumph. He could never become blasé about something which brings him so much pleasure, even if it is not a very lucrative way of keeping the wolf from the door! His family has a small business making tachographs for lorries, for, though he is continually in the top three of the National Drivers Table, he would be hard pushed to keep Theresa and the boys solely on his earnings as a driver.

Though he agrees that the future of the sport lies on the hard tracks, he is keen that there should not be a monopoly, and has a very special place in his heart for the grass circuits, particularly Appleby and Tregaron. Though anybody witnessing Alan's important victories could be left in no doubt as to how much he enjoys them, it isn't always the obvious ones that have given him the most pleasure. Naturally, Golden Dale is a favourite with Alan, but then so was a horse called Perfect Pick. 'He had a serious kink when he came to us and would run off the track if the mood took him. But Theresa spent a lot of time making a pet of him and he won at Appleby for us before being sold to Canada where he went 1.56.' Stay Cool is another horse who is lodged in Alan's affections, winning both days at Appleby in 1985, and proving that Alan was indeed a driver to be reckoned with, heralding an upward surge in his career. Nowadays he and Staffordshire trainer, Brian Mould, make a very formidable team.

In October 1992, Alan was the first driver to pilot five winners at a meeting at Tir Prince Raceway, though he had previously driven six winners from six drives at Kendal despite having a plaster cast on his leg. This fracture occurred when a cart collapsed, though he also broke a leg when a horse reared over on him, and his wrist has also been a casualty. 'It was my own fault I broke it,' he related cheerfully, 'I was in front in a race and looked round to see where the opposition was instead of looking where I was going!' Alan Haythornthwaite's ambitions are quite simple – to keep 'firing to the wire' in front and 'keep doing good'. But, win or lose, the spontaneous smile is there, and his continuing success belies the old adage, 'Nice guys finish last.'

Evelyn Slack

Evelyn Hogarth rode her first winner in a pony race at the age of eight, wearing her best frilly frock. 'Mother was fed up of my sisters and I looking like tomboys, and we always had to dress up to go out, and someone asked me to ride this pony when I was at the local sports . . .'

Evelyn was born and bred to 'trotting' and rode her first winner under that code at the age of fourteen on a little mare called Barbara M, who once won nine races in a week. Because she has been on the scene most of her life, she has never even considered her gender, let alone found it a disadvantage. As for equality, Evelyn laughs. 'I was driving when most of today's drivers were in diapers!' In 1962 she married Arthur Slack and together they founded the Stoneriggs Stud, producing class performers, many of which Evelyn trains and drives.

There is no doubt that Evelyn is a tough lady. She more than holds her own at the highest level in the sport, yet has three little granddaughters. It would be easy to imagine Evelyn Slack as a 'macho' woman, but the truth is that she is a lady. Her gentle Cumbrian accents are so soft that you have to strain your ears to catch them, and her pleasure in her horses bespeak her as an absolutely genuine, truly likeable person.

Stoneriggs Merc, the 1993 BHRC Horse Of The Year, is the current gem in Evelyn's string, but she has had the pleasure of many splendid animals, including Stoneriggs Kid, Kestrel, Limited and Inmate, and the magnificent mare, Monkroyd Mystery. She won fifty-two races in three seasons for the Slacks before retiring to the breeding paddocks, and Evelyn reckons she is so far the best she has had the pleasure of driving, because it didn't matter what the race surface or distance was, she would win. 'She really was something else, and recorded six mile races under 2.1.0. She'd just go for ever. Merc may catch her up yet, but she was certainly something different.'

Evelyn's daughter, Diane, and son, Kenneth, have both followed her tyre tracks into the winners' circle, and Diane, who also helps with the horses at Stoneriggs, has ridden under National Hunt rules for her mother, who also holds a permit to train in the Thoroughbred world. 'Diane rode Megan's Move to win at Sedgefield, but we didn't have another runner really until

Tighter Budget won at Hexham for us at 33–1, five years later.'

In 1982, Evelyn became a registered farrier, and now shoes all her own horses. 'Taking that exam was the most nerve-wracking thing I've ever done in my life! I'd spent every spare minute in the farrier's shops in Canada, but when that top man came up from London as my examiner, I think I learned more in the three hours he was with me than I had all the rest of the time put together!' she recalled. Being able to shoe her own horses is a real godsend, since farriery is such a vital facet of action and performance in harness racing. What suits a horse best to get him pacing clean and fast is often a case of trial and error, so Evelyn can experiment with different plates and ideas until she finds the key.

Since she has won so very many races and championships, one could be forgiven for wondering if Evelyn still got a buzz from winning. But there is no doubt that she finds every victory a magic one. 'It's just lovely hitting that winning post first, a marvellous sensation! I really do appreciate every winner, because, you never know, there may not be another. And of course it's only natural to be a little disappointed when you get beat, but then I look at the winner and think, "Well, pal, I know just what that feels like!" and I feel better about it because someone else is enjoying that pleasure.'

Overdale is another horse who is dear to Evelyn. 'He was a lovely drive. You could almost throw your reins at him and he would sit his chin on the helmet of the driver in front. But once you eased him over, you had to be sure there was room to go, because once he went, there was no stopping him!'

Bob Kennedy

Ian Armstrong once said of Bob Kennedy, 'You could live two lifetimes and never meet another man like him!' This is an understatement! A dour Scot, living not too far from Corbiewood Stadium, Bob has devoted most of his very full life to 'trotting'. Both his father and grandfather raced harness horses, and Bob has owned winners in many different countries. His class trotter, Mark Lobell, who runs in the colours of Bob's daughter, Caroline, has won in Germany, after a lucrative campaign on the British circuits, and Bob has plans now to try him in Russia.

Over the years, he has owned class horses such as Dark Orator and Yankee Bill, and currently Surprise Skipper, Little Airman and Rainmaker have kept him a familiar figure in the winners' enclosure.

Bob can often be seen driving around in a van with a replica of a horse and sulky on the roof, complete with a sign urging attendance at Corbiewood. He does this completely of his own volition, keen that all should

Owner Bob Kennedy with Jim McInally, his son Paul, and Mandy Stanley, with Little Airman at Corbiewood.

taste the delights of the sport which has provided him with so many triumphs and tragedies.

Because of his offbeat approach to life, Bob has occasionally outraged those at the helm of BHRC, but he works on the theory that all publicity is good publicity. Over the years he has built and promoted eight different tracks, and spent vast fortunes in attempting to market harness racing in the most unorthodox manner. 'The shoemaker's bairn is always the worst shod!' he pointed out in his soft Scottish lilt with its overtones of Canadian drawl. (He has spent a considerable time in Canada, where his horses have won 110 races). 'The people within the sport need to push it but they don't . . .'

Bob's bids for airplay have few boundaries. When he was getting too few people through the gate for his meetings at one Scottish track, he shipped six horses and the start-car to Princes Street in Edinburgh. Stopping the traffic, he staged an impromptu race, and was duly arrested for a public disorder offence. The case in court was much publicized, and he may have been fined £50, but his track was full to capacity the following Saturday.

He was also one of the first men to run a race meeting on a Sunday, which scandalized the police force and sent them hot-foot to Craigmulloch Trotting Track to implement the betting and gaming laws. Bob refused to let any of the officers in without paying, which they eventually did, and he even made the Detective Inspector pay five shillings to become a member of his 'club'! The crowd were enjoying their day out immensely, and Bob got round most of the difficulties by tying bingo tickets on all the horses' bridles and making anyone who had struck a winning bet shout 'House!' Despite the continued attentions of the law, he managed to stage a few of these very popular Sabbath meetings by registering the track as a club, which would be entitled to run a lottery. This had to be done weekly, and Bob finally had his collar felt when he eventually forgot to send in his £2.00 fee, and the fun had to stop.

'The things I've done for "trotting"!' he exclaimed, and went on to relate how he invented the ghost of Motherwell Raceway. In fact a horse called Lucky Miller had indeed died near there when he had slipped into a hole in his field. So Bob spread the word that he had seen an unearthly horse galloping up the Motherwell track, snorting fire. Much was written in the press about 'sightings' of the ghost horse over the weeks, culminating in a midnight seance on the track.

Bob Kennedy loves the unusual. When his stallion, Rainmaker, won at Corbiewood with Jim McInally in the winter of 1993, Bob appeared to collect his rosette in an outfit that included his customary Stetson, ornate rowelled spurs and a Count of Monte Cristo cape. He had originally planned to drive to the winners' enclosure in his Rolls Royce, but had been too busy backing his convictions. So great had his confidence been in the horse that he had not deigned to back him to win, but was staking substantial wagers that he would do so by an excess of five lengths. Rainmaker obliged by eight.

Bob has a real weakness for skewbalds and piebalds, and his Dry Ginger once recorded 2.06 at Kendal to become the fastest coloured horse in the country. Every Christmas he visits Corbiewood dressed as Santa Claus, in a cart behind his coloured cob, and gives sweets away to all the children at the meeting.

Bob Kennedy has spent fortunes on his beloved sport over the years, and, even if his methods are not exactly orthodox, without his promotions, the world of harness racing would be a much poorer place.

Clem Dodd

If harness racing had received the recognition that it had deserved, Clem Dodd would be as familiar a name as Lester Piggott. Now in his seventies, Clem is one of the oldest supporters of the sport, along with Jack Bousefield. He was National Champion Driver for the final time when he was well into his sixties, and was the last man to go through the card, driving the winner of every race, and was unlucky not to do so on two consecutive occasions. A spry, polite man, he is still consumed by his passion for his sport and has a

Cole Star, winner of the 1965 Musselburgh Famous Pace, driven by Clem Dodd, in a workout at home in Derbyshire.

wealth of memories of top class horses winning the very best races all over the country.

Clem Dodd's late uncle, George, and cousin, Edmund, were also great trainers and drivers in their day, and George was also the promoter of racing at Droylsden. It was obvious that Clem would also be interested in the sport, and he rode his first winner at the age of thirteen, in 1929. His visits to the winners' enclosure were to continue for another fifty years, and he has won every important race in the British Isles on numerous occasions. Clem calculates that he has won thirteen important races at Musselburgh since he made his debut there in 1932 with Dan's Son, excluding heats. He has never counted up his Appleby winners, and began to fondly recollect them, 'Hanover Way, Young Morecombe, Starlight . . . Young Steven should have won it but got blinded by dust, it was a very dry year and he had very sensitive eyes . . . April Star and Pleasant Surprise of the Bousefields, Golden Sun, Donald Pimlott's Scotch Silk . . . he was commentator at the Manchester track. That was a good three-year-old that got sold to America . . . my favourite, Gala Queen, one in a lifetime, she was, oh, and Young Demon. He came from New Zealand where he'd been in a bad accident, and he was a nervous wreck . . . we had to keep a sheep with him for company. But he could move, he floated! Coming out of the back straight at Appleby, he had such a long stride that he went past the field in about four steps, and the crowd up on the bank all gasped as one and stood up, he was that impressive . . .'

All who were lucky enough to watch Clem Dodd on the sulky realized that they were watching a master of his art. 'He just seemed to sit there and horses used to run for him!' explained his son-in-law, John Towe, but Clem's talent was apparently almost a tangible thing. Many older spectators claim that today's drivers are not in the same league, and that Clem was a horseman through and through.

Clem loved the mare Gala Queen in particular, though he had a special fondness for Cole's Star, Ellen Mary, Starlight and Young Morecombe. And Outlaw was very special, competing until he was well into his twenties. 'He won at Hawes as a three-year-old, and at twenty-three!'

Clem naturally has a million tales to tell, but loves to speak of a little coloured mare that he raced, named Jane Eyre. She belonged to a millionaire called Dick Hampton, who prided himself on his thriftiness, even to the point of carrying a bottle of cold tea in his pocket so he would never need to buy a cup at 'The Trots'! Bill Cole, Ted's (of the Golden Future Stud) father, had bought a horse with a big reputation to the races, and it was well fancied, though Clem was adamant that Jane Eyre had a good chance. And so it proved, because the gutsy little mare, 'always a glutton for punishment', won the heat and then battled home to take the Final. 'Bill Cole was real surprised, pushing his cap back, scratching his head and looking at his good horse as Ted led it away, and Dick Hampton couldn't help himself, he went across to Bill and said, "Ah, Bill, thee and thy million-dollar 'orses! That pony cost me twelve pound!" '

Clem Dodd has undoubtedly crammed several lifetimes into one, and probably forgotten more about horses and harness racing than most of us will ever know.

Naturally, for all the true characters of the sport to be recorded in these pages, the Sowerbys, Stricklands, Harrops, Higginses, Lees, etc., the book would rival *War and Peace* for length. The rich colour that they add is part of the potent and fatal attraction of harness racing.

Starlight, one of Clem Dodd's favourite horses, winning at Chesterfield rugby ground in the late 1950s.

12

Look! No Hopples!

In the early days, probably right up until the 1960s, there were many more of the diagonally gaited horses contesting races with pacers in the UK than there are now. Many trotters belonged to tradesmen in the 1920s and 30s, their speed at delivering goods being of vital importance. Many of the official harness racing fixtures were then held on Monday afternoons, particularly in the Manchester area, as this was half-day closing for the shopkeepers, who utilized it to take their ponies to do battle on the circuits.

Some of the older devotees of harness racing have been heard to sniff that the sport 'Ain't like it used to be'; they are referring to the gradual decline in popularity of diagonally gaited horses, mainly due to pacers being approximately three seconds a mile faster. A good pacer will usually beat a good trotter in an open race, and so keeping a trotter for the few races restricted to them only is not a particularly viable proposition.

There is a great deal of skill attached to driving a square trotter, keeping him balanced and fluent in his gait, and the die-hards are proud of their expertise. Certainly the talents of such drivers as Edmund, George and Clem Dodd, Jim Pickard, Jimmy Young, Bill and Snowy Evans and Davie Douglas (who still holds the UK two-mile record) in the past were without question.

Attention to shoeing is crucial to any harness racehorse, but especially so with trotters who often need weight on their toes to balance their strides and help find their correct rhythm. So a good farrier is worth his weight in gold!

The trotting gait comprises an equal and even extension backward and forward of the four moving legs. Any irregular extension of any leg/s results in a faulty gait, and probably interference. It is here that proper shoeing and balancing can remedy the situation. When the trotter is at full stretch, his hind limbs are the 'pistons' that provide the driving force that propels him forward. The fore-legs, rolling over in a fluid rhythm, are the 'balance-wheels', and establish the basic nature of the gait. There is a great deal of knee and hock action in trotting, but too much can waste energy and inefficiently cover the ground. Due to the very nature of this action, there is a possibility that a trotter may knock his own elbows, or catch the following hind leg with a front foot at speed. This is why they often wear tough leather boots to protect these, and other, areas.

There are two basic gait types among trotters, the 'line' gait, where the horse carries the front and hind leg in a direct line when viewed from the front or rear, and the 'passing' gaited trotter, where he places the hind leg slightly outside the fore-leg when in motion. There is little difference in the performance of the two, though some trainers prefer the latter because they usually find their speed more quickly.

Trotting is the only permissible gait in European countries, and most of the diagonally gaited horses competing in Great Britain today have been imported. The bloodlines of the trotter are very similar to that of the pacer, going back to the splendid American stallions Messenger, Hambletonian and Peter The Great. Axeworthy, Scotland and Volomite are all significant sires in the pedigrees of trotters.

Most European countries have introduced this American blood in an attempt to improve their own breed, and in fact so alarming was the export of good American trotting stallions and mares that the phrase, 'Will the last trotter to leave the country please put the lights out?' has become frequent badinage on the scene in the USA. The Russians, too, have utilized good American bloodlines to bring speed to the inherent stamina of their Orlov breed.

The French, though, have developed their own breeding lines which do not include Hambletonian (or at least not on the male side), their stud book having been closed to American-bred stock since 1937. These lines, however, do descend from the Godolphin Arab and the Darley Arabian through the Thoroughbred, Rattler. The most significant male influences on the bloodlines of the French trotter are considered to have been Normand, Fuschia and Phaeton. In comparison to the breed in other countries, the French performers are much bigger and stronger types. Genetically speaking, the breeding of a trotter is no simple task. The pacing gait is generally dominant over the trotting gait, so that when a pacer is bred to a trotter, the resulting foal is practically always a pacer. Ninety-nine per cent of the time a pacer bred to a pacer produces a pacing offspring, but perversely, a trotter bred to a trotter can also often produce a pacer! Breeding is frequently something of a lottery (the late Mac Higgins, a real character in the dealing world, used to quote, 'Fools breed 'em for wise men to buy 'em') but this complication must have breeders reaching for the valium!

BHRC trotter of the year, Gustav Way, driven by Stevie Lees.

The BHRC Trotter Of The Year in 1993 was George Carter's Gustav Way (Smokin Yankee/Elvira Way). The Swedish-bred eight-year-old, expertly handled by ex-showjumper, Helen Keyes, won five good races to take the title. The partnership of Carter–Keyes is a formidable one on the square-gaited scene, for they are also responsible for the Danish-bred Jaques Bilto (Stanley Cup/Jaqueline Axeworthy), who set a new National record of 2.40.5 over a mile and a quarter in 1992 when driven by the gifted Ian Pimlott. Other owners and trainers such as Trevor Barton, Peter Lee, Bill Green and Darren Piccolo devote their racing attentions to trotters, while others such as Tony Cotton are happy to deal with both gaits.

Many track promoters are beginning to frame trotting races to encourage support from across the English Channel, so that French owners send horses over to be trained at the circuits. Jane Paterson, leading lady trainer at Tir Prince Raceway, recorded a string of wins in 1993 with French imports, mostly driven by Johnny Blissett, crack pilot of the diagonal gait.

Prior to 1994, the Classic races of the trotting calendar were the Roosevelt Cup, the Prakas Championship and the Prakas Derby.

In 1993, trotting only accounted for 5 per cent of races and prize money. But with the formation of the new society, TROTBritain, a revolution on the trotting scene has occurred, and a programme of Classic, Championship and circuit races is planned, including events for the much neglected young trotters. TROTBritain, the brainchild of BHRC Liaison Officer, Dr Jack Dowie, who is the inaugural chairman, is dedicated to the advancement of the square-gaited trotter within British harness racing. A non-profit-making society, TROTBritain also aims to establish a trotting stud book, give awards to breeders, trainers and drivers, and expand links with Europe in the hope that trotting can again become a significant part of harness racing in the UK. With Richard Muddle planning to include three trotting races on each card at Dunstall Park, increased opportunities for the square-gaited performers are imminent.

A trotter in full flight is indeed an inspiring sight. There are several brilliant competitors in the square-gaited events, and most of them have to overcome long handicap deficits, as there are not enough horses to regularly stage trotting Free-for-Alls. Tony Cotton's American-bred stallion, Jeff's Comfort (Cold Comfort/Regal Heather), ran up a sequence of victories in 1993 to become a maximum handicapped horse (off an eighty-yard trail). He had overcome many problems on his way to the winners' circle, having been badly kicked in the face prior to Tony purchasing him, which had made it difficult for him to tolerate a bit in his mouth.

Bill Edwards's Mr Will (Den.) (Super Lance/Tahiti Sporup) is a firm favourite with the Tir Prince crowd, as are Darren Piccolo's Noble Crown (Den.) (Advertiser/Atalja), Peter Mather's Star Trade (Hol.) (Sonja's Boy/Saunders Speedster) and the grand veteran Winston (Hol.) (Kameraad/Janinike B). Little Erster (Ersters Boy/Saunders Investiture), who won the 1993 Prakas Championship with Bob Lees, is currently the best British-bred trotter on the circuits, and Trevor Barton's Evelyn Hazelhaar (Hol.) (Uno Hazelhaar/Tivoli Hazelhaar) is the most consistent mare. Other top-class contestants are UK record holder Ideal Key (Swe.) (Ideal De Gazeau/Madam Key), Lord Ixa (Den.) (Lord Valentine/Fame To C), dual-Musselburgh winner Emerald Empire (Here/Red Silk), Xola Budd (Native Starlight/Oradea) and Yoboko Du Bois (Hol.) (Rislip Wind/Jonia Du Bois). The recent Swedish import, Prometheus Pay, has also made his mark, and 'won' the first televised exhibition race at Dunstall Park in January, 1994.

Little Erster (Bob Lees) (centre) *en route to success in a trot at Tir Prince.*

The Irish-bred Mark Lobell (Slyheel (USA)/Lady Rep), a former winner of the Prakas Derby, has had a successful campaign in Germany for Caroline Kennedy, following an impressive return to the UK tracks after a freak injury. The gelding actually had his tongue bitten off by another horse when they were in adjacent stables. He owes much of his recovery to the meticulous nursing of Jane Paterson's daughter, Nicky, who spent much of her time ensuring that he swallowed the gruel she had prepared for him.

The UK mile record for trotters is currently held by the Danish-bred Igen Bork, who recorded 2.03.4 in 1991. This again reflects how British performance compares with those in America, where the conditions are much more favourable for fast times. The first trotter in the world to break the two-minute barrier was Lou Dillon in America in 1903, clocking 1.58.1/2. The famous grey gelding, Greyhound, one of the toughest of trotters, recorded a world record of 1.55.1/4 almost forty years later, illustrating that trotting is a serious business in the USA. The Triple Crown of America's square-gaited circuits consists of the Classic races, The Hambletonian, the Kentucky Futurity and The Yonkers Trot. Such is the keen competition amongst the diagonally gaited contenders that the last horse to win the Triple Crown was Superbowl in 1972. Mack Lobell, Napolitano, Pine Chip and American Winner are amongst other top performers on the trotting roll of honour 'across the pond'.

In France, trotting is possibly even more popular than its Thoroughbred counterpart, and the multi-storeyed stadium at Vincennes, on the outskirts of Paris, is quite breathtaking. Certainly, the betting turnover on races such as the Pris D'Amérique is among the most lucrative in the world. The Societé d'Encouragement à l'élévage du Cheval Francais (SECF) is the governing body of the sport in France, and is keen to support the furthering of trotting in the UK. It has expressed much interest in the society TROTBritain, accepting the invitation to become an associate member.

Relations with the Netherlands were strengthened by an International Challenge in 1993, where Dutch drivers visited Tir Prince Raceway for a series of races, and British drivers were invited to compete at Nootdorp, in Holland. The British drivers emerged the victors of the challenge, and were excellent ambassadors for the sport in the UK. Hopefully, now the basics are in place to encourage the breeding, owning and racing of square trotters, their popularity will rekindle on the British scene, thus delighting the supporters who profess themselves 'hot to trot'!

13

Saddle Races

Saddle races are always a popular spectacle with harness-racing crowds. Prior to the change in the National Handicapping system in the early 1990s, there was generally one at the end of most grass fixtures, but, sadly, they are now few and far between. Prior to the 1960s, riding harness race-horses against driven horses in the same race was quite acceptable, and the light jockeys were very popular. In France, several of the races on each card are ridden, and there are some valuable events, such as the Prix de la Président de la République, which are run under saddle.

Now no horse under BHRC rules is permitted to take part in a saddle race unless it is of Open Handicap class, and has earlier competed at the meeting in a sulky. A licence to ride in saddle races will be granted by the BHRC to applicants who have attained their 14th birthday, and who have completed a ridden test-race to the satisfaction of the stewards. A driving licence also covers riding in saddle races.

Most of the harness is the same as used on the horse when in the cart, except that the saddle replaces the pad. There has to be a ring fitted to both the pommel and cantle of the saddle to attach the overcheck and the crupper. Most jockeys use light racing saddles, and any saddler will fix the rings, which entails the saddle being taken apart and a strong piece of webbing attaching the rings to the actual tree.

The middle hopple-hanger runs over the top of the saddle, and the rider should take care not to dig a toe or heel underneath it when kicking for home!

The bridle is obviously the same one that the horse customarily wears, with normal reins attached, the rubber-gripped racing variety being best, for horses can pull very hard under saddle, and keeping hold of their heads to help balance them is even more crucial. In France this problem is

Welsh classic saddle race at Tregaron 1993. (Left to right) *Shantel (Shane Ward), Bernard Shore (Jackie Williams), Stoneriggs Herbie (the author), Banacec (Linda Evans) and Ynys Stirling (Keith Young).*

addressed by fearsome-looking ironmongery in the horses' mouths, but luckily this is not practised in the UK. There are different methods of riding a laterally gaited horse, some sit and some rise, though the time-honoured way is to sit and lean slightly back. However, many modern exponents of the art such as Alex Lees and Nicky Cabb adopt a crouched, forward position, not unlike a flat jockey. Some horse relish the under-saddle events and run consistently well in them. Robo, Kane, Factory Joe, Rhiewstar, Bernard

Shore and the 1993 Tregaron Saddle Race victor, Banacec, are all tough contenders.

Ex-point-to-point jockey, Jackie Williams is a specialist in the saddle events of Wales and the West, and in 1992 contested five races, winning four and being placed on the other occasion. Most of the riders are females, including Joanne Taff, Linda Evans, Debbie and Angela Dyer, Lesley Richards and Vicki Harris, but there are a handful of lightweight male jockeys, Keith Young, David Bevan and Shane Ward among them.

Prior to 1994, a win under saddle was only handicapped in saddle races, and was not applied to races in the sulky, but a saddle-race victory is now counted in all starts. This alteration further causes the decline of saddle races, since the prize money on offer is considerably less than for a normal Open Handicap event.

Tradition will undoubtedly prevent under-saddle events from disappearing completely, and rightly so, for the sake of those who have talented skills in the saddle and are light enough to use them to their best advantage.

14

The Future – from Footlights to Floodlights

Come hell or high water, there will always be harness racing in the UK. With the right attitude of its competitors, and the marketing skills of its promoters, it should at last be going *somewhere* – and at a two-minute rate. In the early 1990s, 'Wolverhampton' was the word on every supporter's lips, for the development at Dunstall Park promised both opportunities and airplay for the sport. There is no doubt that Dunstall Park intends harness racing to expand rapidly as it heads for the 21st century, and we hope it will become a serious off-track betting medium.

The Dunstall Park executive are definitely thinking in the long term, for, with an eye on the future, they have included the British Harness Racing School in their scheme. The main aim of this school is to provide young people with a broad introduction to working with horses, and to nurture the basic skills relevant to the harness-racing industry. Under the tuition of Brian Peachey, students work towards a national vocational certificate in basic horsecare. When a student successfully completes a course, the school will try to find a placement for him or her with a professional trainer. Four-day trials are offered to students, though the actual courses are generally twelve weeks in length.

The sport boasts many young enthusiasts. Spectators in Wales and the West are often treated to the sight of young Alexander Cotton in full regalia with his Shetland pony in his custom-built sulky trotting round the lorry park while his father speeds around the circuits. And the future of the sport certainly seems secure enough with a healthy contingent of young drivers who are already making their mark on the result sheets.

Barry Neal, who is a garage owner from Manchester, is a recent recruit to the scene. He is the nephew of ace driver, Ian Pimlott, and had previously been a regular spectator until he could bear it no longer and had to try it for himself. He bought the class campaigner, Staly TT, from Ian, and Greenfold Pride, a youngster. Only his second drive saw him in the winners' enclosure at Tir Prince, and he has been a regular there ever since. He stables his horses with Bill Green at Manchester, and is keen to enjoy even greater success. He was awarded the Leading Young Driver award at Tir Prince in 1993, scoring ten times in his first season.

Willie Greenhorn Jnr ensured that his mother, Janet, took the 1993 Leading Owner Award to Scotland with his outstanding successes on the sulky seat. His 21 victories earned him a 24 per cent strike rate, and his winter racing record with the brilliant horses, Stoneriggs Jet and Stephen's Cover, was especially notable. Tall and quiet, he occasionally hands the reins to his brother, Alan, when he qualifies two horses for a Final, and it is not an uncommon sight for the Greenhorn brothers to be battling it out up the stretch.

Billy Williams Jnr is an ebullient, likeable character who has been voted Young Driver Of The Year on a couple of occasions since taking out his driving licence at sixteen years of age. He has been in most of the British teams who have been involved in International challenges, and capably handles both trotters and pacers. He is a familiar figure at Tir Prince where he good-humouredly assists his father in the running of the raceway.

Irishman, James Murdock, is another talented young driver based at Tir Prince, where he also trains. His successes on the hard tracks and the grass circuits keep him consistently in the top six of the national driver's table.

Paul Evans, a convert from the 'galloping' circuits, is one of the up-and-coming drivers on the circuits of Wales and the West. His first couple of drives took him into the placings, and his first winner was Raceover Jack at Walton. He proved himself as a force to be noted by later recording the fastest time of the day at Huntley when victorious with Frank Morlidge's good mare Just Penny. Paul then went on to clock 2.9.0 at Weobley with Raceover Jack, one of the fastest grass times of the season in the region. Leckwith Dancer, Ollie Hill's promising two-year-old, also obliged impressively and set Paul on the quest for a Classic win.

David Bevan, who graduated to driving in Wales and the West after successfully contesting saddle races, also recorded several wins in his first season on the sulky seat. George and William Drysdale, who help run the family farm and stud near Alloa, both drive their full quota of winners on the Scottish circuits, and have made their mark in prestigious events throughout the UK. Both brothers are track record holders, George, the elder, holds Corbiewood's record with McGuigan, while Willie smashed Errol Raceway's best time with Armbro Fling in 1993 on two occasions. The

Young Clare Bousefield, who is in the top rank of lady drivers, on her home ground at Appleby.

brothers certainly enjoy their forays to Tregaron and beyond, raising the Scottish flag at most of the major fixtures. Diane and Clare Bousefield, Shane Lee, John Ball Jnr, Mark Kennedy, Sara Mould, Shane Dyer, Danielle Stimpson, Libby Lloyd, John Towe Jnr and Shane Ward, among many others, ensure that young drivers are well represented in the ranks. But with luck there will be new owners, trainers and drivers of all ages among the new recruits as word of the sport's excitement and attraction spreads. Much of this attraction is due to the live television coverage of floodlit meetings from Tir Prince by S4C. The transmissions have a huge following, and the coverage of a special meeting in September, 1993, won a coveted BAFTA Cymru award for the Mapp Television team. Since the nominations included such established events as The Five Nations Rugby series, this was certainly a great fillip for the sport.

Since the turn of the century, harness racing has been quietly jogging along in the shadow cast by other equestrian activities. But now, the sport of Lords, if not of Kings, is set to pace briskly forward to take its rightful place under the floodlights; its hitherto unsung heroes can take a well earned bow.

Names and Addresses

The Tracks

Tir Prince Raceway
Towyn Road, Towyn, Aberegele, Clwyd LL22 9NW
contact: Billy Williams or Wendy Fairclough
tel. 0745 345123 fax 0745 331829

Corbiewood
contact: Ian Armstrong, Armstrong Printing Ltd, Lornshill, Alloa FK10 2EX

York Raceway
contact: Shelagh Jackson, 55 Beech Grove, Acombe, York YO2 5DY
tel. 0904 799352 or 0423 330084 (Raceway)

Amman Valley Trotting Club
contact: Mrs A. Launchbury, The Post Office, Llyncelwyn Road, Tairgwaith, Ammanford, Dyfed
tel. 0269 823288

Appleby Spring Races
Secretary: David Gray, Kangaroo House, Colby, Cumbria CA16 6BR
tel. 07683 51256

Musselburgh
contact: Carole Auld, Stable Cottage, Top Row, Elphinstone, Tranent EH2 2LS
tel. 0875 340325

Wreningham (c/o East Anglia Harness Racing Association, *see below*)
tel. 0508 471201

Tregaron Trotting Club
contact: Raymond and Carole Jenkins, Bryniethin, Tyn-y-Graig, Ystrad Meurig, Dyfed
tel. 0974 3343

Dunstall Park
Gorsebrook Road, Dunstall, Wolverhampton
contact: Mick Wilcox or Kathy Bratt
tel. 0543 360868 (home) 0543 480476 (racecourse) 0902 24481

Associations

UKHRA
Secretary: Elisabeth Towe, 99 Smedley St, Matlock, Derbyshire
tel. 0629 582062

BHRC
Secretary: Anne Brophy, Bryn Goleu, Bryniau, Dyserth, Rhyl, Clwyd LL18 6ER
tel. 0745 854746

Eden Valley Trotting Association
Secretary: Mrs S. Barr, 36 Castle View, Brough, Kirkby Stephen, Cumbria CA17 4BA

Wales and the West Harness Racing Association
Secretary: Heulwen Thomas, Delfryn, Llwnpiod, Llangeitho, Tregaron, Dyfed SY25 6TA
tel. 0974 298089

British Harness Racecourse Association
contact: Billy Williams/Wendy Fairclough, Tir Prince Raceway, Towyn Road, Towyn, Aberegele, Clwyd LL22 9NW
tel. 0745 345123 fax 0745 331829

Scottish Trotting Horse Owners Association
Secretary: Alistair Smith, 1 Brookfield Place, Alva FK12 5AB
tel. 0259 60177

TROTBritain
Secretary: Elisabeth Blazak, Flaxlands Farm, Roade Lane, Charlton Roade, Norwich NR16 1RQ
tel. 0953 789367

Grass Track Association
Secretary: Una Forrest, 5 Raby Moor, Cockfield, Bishops Auckland, Co. Durham DL13 5HG

East Anglian Harness Racing Association
Secretary: Elaine Oliver, 22 Convent Garden Road, Caister-on-Sea, Great Yarmouth
tel. 0493 377277

North-east Standardbred Association
Secretary: Una Forrest, 5 Raby Moor, Cockfield, Bishops Auckland, Co Durham DL13 5HG

Witton Castle Harness Racing Club
Secretary: Murray Marton, 5 Side (Rear), Newcastle-upon-Tyne
tel. 091 2322000

British Harness Racing School
Pamela McKenna, Dunstall Park, Gorsebrook Road, Dunstall, Wolverhampton
tel. 0902 24481

Weatherby's
BHRC Dept, Sanders Road, Wellingborough, NN8 4BX
tel. 0933 440077 ext 235

Index